His love endures

Eagle's Wings

Eagle's Wings

Laura McDonald

Covenanters

Published by
Covenanters Press

an imprint of
Zeticula
57 St Vincent Crescent
Glasgow
G3 8NQ

http://www.covenanters.co.uk
admin@covenanters.co.uk

Text Copyright © Laura McDonald 2006
www.lauramcdonald.co.uk

All photographs © Laura McDonald 2006
Cover design © Laura McDonald 2006

ISBN 1 905022 28 X Paperback

Contents

Acknowledgements

First and foremost, my deepest gratitude and all my love goes to God, my Father in Heaven, in whom I have discovered a life that is worth the living, love that knows no bounds and with Him anything is possible. Thank you for believing in me, being so patient with me and for pretty much everything!

My sisters, all of you are not only my sisters but my friends and I am so glad God gave us each other. You are all unique as our relationships but together 'we are family'. Thanks for being a part of my life and making it sparkle - I truly love you all to bits!

My family, you have given me places to eat, talk, sleep, talk, rest, talk, cry, talk – you have blown me away with your love and support, bramble jelly and empire biscuits! Thank you, for you have made my world a better place by being in it!

My bestest pal in the whole wide world – you truly are a friend who 'sticks closer than a brother' and who has 'loved at ALL times'. You're amazing in every way – your friendship is such an amazing gift to me for which I will be eternally grateful.

My friends who have travelled the world with me, shared an office with me, taken me for 'drives', kept me supplied with movies, hugged me, sent me cards, emailed me, run on the beach with me, danced with me, sang with me, played guitar with me, had me over for barbecues, showed me how to use 'power tools', provided me with firewood, helped me with my home PC, encouraged me and have 'lent an ear' – I want to thank you for your friendship, for you have all played a part in my life and enhanced it just by being you, and I can honestly say, because of you, I am blessed!

All at East Gate Church for being such a supportive bunch and to which the above applies. Arthur, thank you for encouraging me always – our logo says it all - It is a new day!

To all of you I say a hearty thank you, and pray God will bless your socks right off!

Eagle's Wings

You found me in the wilderness
Afraid and alone
You found me in the wasteland
Of my life
You wrapped Your arms around me
And showed me what to do
You gave me hope
You gave me love
You gave me life

You carried me on eagle's wings
Through my darkest night
You kept me in safety
And soared me to the heights
You held me close beside You
And taught my heart to sing
O God I am so grateful
For eagle's wings

Deuteronomy 32:10-12 says:

'He found them in a desert land, in an empty, howling wasteland. He surrounded them and watched over them; he guarded them as his most precious possession. Like an eagle that rouses her chicks and hovers over her young, so he spread his wings to take them in and carried them aloft on his pinions. The Lord alone guided them; they lived without any foreign gods,' (NLT)

This was my very first 'real' song that I wrote based upon these verses and this is the basis for the title of this book although as you read through the poems, the theme of a 'loosed' bird comes through.

God found me and cared enough not to leave me in that howling wasteland of my life and I have discovered that I am His most precious possession…as too are you and eagle's wings will carry us through that wasteland to the highlands!

Foreword

Have you ever said, 'this is not what I planned for my life' or 'this is not how I thought it would be'?

In January 2005 I found myself in a place I never thought I would ever be. I had been praying fervently for my husband and truly believed God was going to turn things around in our marriage. Even upon discovering my husband's unfaithfulness I still hoped our relationship was not at an end. We had come through three very hard years and I thought the worst was over. With hindsight I can see that during these three years God had been preparing me for this day – I just hadn't known it. For in those three years of preparation, through a journey of vulnerability and sometimes such rawness I felt I would surely die, I discovered things about myself. I was broken, stripped and hurting and many times I wanted to give up on life. Then to discover the affair and witness the end of my marriage – the sheer agony and wrenching apart of my being was beyond anything I had ever experienced - but God kept me through it all. Now less than two years on I find myself in a place I never imagined or dreamed; a place of peace and rest within me I never thought possible!

My story and the poems that follow reveal my journey of discovery; the preparation, the revelation and the healing through the opening of a cage door within my life. It is my hope that, as I share, and as you read my story and poems in the quiet, you too will be encouraged in knowing you are never alone. Maybe you may even hear a key turning in a lock, the clatter of chains as they fall to the ground and the high screech of a prison door being opened in your life. Freedom awaits.

A little explanation

What I've written is not a celebration of divorce, nor freedom from marriage/relationships. It is not a man-hating crusade – far from it. I do not hate the man to whom I was married, I loved him passionately and unconditionally and I continue to pray that God will bring him to a place of freedom. I believe both of us could have reached the place I find myself in today, for we are all given free choice in this world in which we live.

The freedom I speak of is freedom from:

Fear of man
Fear of life
Fear of the unknown
Fear of unchartered territory
Fear of change
Fear of failure
Fear of rejection
Fear of abandonment.

When I say God spoke to me, He did this through:

His word, the Bible
Friends/family
Songs/poems
A still quiet voice within me (like when an idea comes to mind).

When I speak of the enemy, this refers to satan, the devil, or whatever you call him. His mission is to steal, kill and destroy and he will use whatever he can — your thoughts, mindsets, your past, etc, — to keep you bound, chained, alone and miserable.

Prayer is talking to God, taking time to listen too — it invites Him into the situation, as He will not force Himself upon anyone, but gives us free choice and free will.

My journey's like that of Christopher Columbus; I didn't know where I was going, when I got there I didn't know where I was, and when I returned I didn't know where I'd been, but I do know that it is God who has taught me to live, to learn, and above all, to love.

And so my desire was, and is, to somehow make it out of this relationship/situation emotionally, physically, mentally and spiritually healed and alive. I could not have done this without the King of Heaven being my guide, without His love for me, in surrounding me with friends and family who have at times gone beyond the call of duty, and in the lonely hours, the King Himself has been my comfort and strength when I did not have the will to carry on.

A little background

Ever since I can remember I have wanted to be a good friend, a good wife and a 'mom'. These were my career plans.

In April 1995 I met the 'man of my dreams'. He was tall, dark and handsome. I loved walking/hill walking — so did he. I enjoyed the theatre and although I had never been to an opera or a ballet, I really wanted to go — so did he. I loved the outdoors as did he. It was incredible that he liked all the things I did; we had so much in common! We had the same ideas about marriage, finances, waiting and having a family after 5 years but really no later than my 30th birthday (I wanted to be young enough to keep up) — amazing — what a perfect match!

Given this you will understand why I was apprehensive. It took him many months to 'win me over' as I had been hurt when I was younger and was very wary. Anybody who showed an interest in me was generally handled with great suspicion. He managed to convince me he wasn't leading me up the garden path, winning me over with his love and persistence, and I was so grateful to God — at last I was loved!

He wanted to serve God. He had made mistakes and was open about them but he wanted to put his past behind him and move on — it didn't matter to me, I simply loved him. He was open with his affection, which I'd never experienced, and it made me feel all the more loved.

Everyone commented on how alike we were, 'two peas in a pod', and you rarely saw one of us without the other. We married almost a year to the day of meeting and it was the best day ever — I'd do it all again!

We worked well together as a team and over time we simply loved and adored one another. He could make me laugh and we found that when one of us was down the other would pick us up — we were that irritating 'lovey-dovey' couple for six years. Don't get me wrong, there were many ups and downs and life hit us hard at times but we were always determined to get through it together, believing God would make a way — which He did.

We started our married life homeless, with no jobs, no money, and an old Mini car that needed work. I found a job and managed to get extra shifts. I had IBS which had been relatively mild but became increasingly worse. After six months in homeless accommodation we managed to get our first (rented) flat. We had a mattress, a Breville toastie maker and a portable TV, and we were happy as wee pigs in poo.

Life continued as such, but one of my husband's 'mistakes' caught up with us. He was confirmed to be a father. Although we had both 'known' of the possibility, the confirmation of it hit us both equally hard. He had hoped to leave his past behind him, and I so wanted to have his children, and this news changed him. The subject of children could not be discussed without causing much upset, but I loved him, and a family was not high on the agenda at this point.

Life was good, even with the upsets. We were both working and had started saving to get a 'home of our own'. I had changed jobs and my IBS settled out a bit. We moved to a little village, to an old upstairs cottage flat which desperately needed work but at least it was ours! We worked hard, and didn't really have time to relax, or have the finances to enjoy leisure activities, but we were together, and that was all that mattered. An opportunity came up for me to have the job I'd always wanted, as a PA, so I cautiously jumped at it! We went to church and although we hosted a really successful house group we were not really happy and felt we needed something more. Friends who were starting a new church asked if we would like to go along. Our initial idea was to help out until we found somewhere else to go, but then we realised we'd found our spiritual home and threw ourselves into it.

After four years of marriage we had our first proper 'holiday', in Arran. He was a bit agitated about going away from home but it was manageable; we both needed the break. It had been such a long time since I'd been able to do any walking; I wasn't really prepared when we decided to climb 3,000 feet to Goat Fell. What a laugh! The day started out a beautiful sun-shiny day. Half way up the weather — typical of Scotland — changed to dense fog/mist with rain so hard my joggy bottoms were falling off and the sleeves ripped off my wax jacket! It got to the stage I was crawling up the rock face on my hands and knees. We had to drive back to our hotel in our underwear! That week we wandered the beach, drove across the island and walked the hotel owner's dog round the forest and waterfall trails. We had a beautiful time.

And so life continued...

Our home was all but finished; once a 2-bedroomed run-down dilapidated flat was now a beautiful 3-bedroomed upstairs/downstairs flat with en-suite, fitted kitchen, roll top slipper bathroom with Italian stone cut tiles – the works – it was gorgeous! We were comfortable financially, and I was becoming increasingly like a mother hen. My IBS had miraculously disappeared after my husband and our pastor had prayed for me. For the first time in our marriage, we could eat out and not have to drive the car at 100 mph to get me to a toilet.

Things looked hopeful as he started to come to terms with being a father and we had even been to see his young son — a huge step! Our closest friends had small children and this helped. He had a 'mate' and we all went on holiday abroad together — again there was a little *angst* on the run up to going but once there all was fine.

I was fast approaching 30 and wanted nothing more than to do what we had talked about — start a family and settle down. We had the flat valued for the insurance and council tax and we were amazed. It was worth double what we had paid for it. We talked, and agreed we'd like to get out of a flat, to have our own garden, especially if we were having a family. We started looking for an 'old' property that we could afford to buy outright. It didn't take long and we moved.

Given that we had just spent 5 years on a building site, we decided we would take a breather for a while, a chance to recoup, have a holiday abroad and plan the work, since we had learned valuable lessons in property development. There had been much going on in our lives; church was good, my husband was hoping to train to be a minister and was very active in the fellowship alongside our pastor. I led the worship, we both did youth work and we were both active in any area where we were needed. Work was busy for both of us. We were best friends and our relationship was as 'active' as ever. I still got excited kissing him and would get shy/embarrassed when he made a move – even after six years of marriage, which he found funny.

The Preparation

In April/May 2002 we went to Fuerteventura on a fortnight's holiday. There was more than the usual *angst* on the run up to going away and it appeared that he wasn't going to go. I really needed the break so I was going to go alone if necessary. As it happened, we both went and whilst there I had a 'glimpse' of what he was feeling, not everything, just a bit. As we walked on the beach, I spoke to him of what I'd seen. I said,

> *'you no longer want the same things you had when we met and although you don't want to walk away, things have changed. You've changed, are changing and it reminds me of being a teenager, not sure which direction to take but pushing boundaries all around, afraid to speak of it…'*

I suggested that he take some time out on his own, find a place of his own for 6-12 months. No-one was to know, it was just between us, so he could sort out what he wanted to do and discover 'who he was' and what he wanted. For I sensed, as Frank Sinatra sang, 'there may be trouble ahead'.

He admitted that he hated travelling and didn't want to go abroad anymore – I said that was fine, I wasn't too bothered; we could holiday in the UK.

He hated walking/hill walking – I was fine with that too, I barely had the time anymore and had realised he hated it and that it had been 'a little white lie' on his part.

The thought of going to the opera or a ballet was too much for him – again, I was fine. These were just little things that really didn't matter – I just loved him and wanted him to be happy!

We spoke at length. He didn't want to move out – that was insane. I was being stupid. There were changes he wanted. He wanted to be more involved in the monetary matters of the house, keeping the joint account for bills and have our own bank accounts, with a separate account for all the renovations. Initially I was hurt, as I felt he didn't trust me, but I also felt relief that he would take on this responsibility, as it seemed he was growing up! We made the changes on our return.

Once we were home an earlier situation with the youth work and other personal things made him decide to step back and take some time out from the church. I stepped back from the youth work as it was impossible to continue alone, but I remained in all other areas of church 'service'.

Other than this I carried on, praying for him, asking that he would resolve the situation with those involved, as I was aware these hurdles are sent to test us, and sometimes you just have to push through, wrong or right, leaving it in God's hands. I believed God would help resolve it.

Nothing more was said of our conversation on holiday.

Within a month he was on permanent nightshift. He worked every night — no breaks — and it was really difficult to adjust for both of us. We had rarely been apart and we found it difficult to sleep without the other there. His complete departure from church life took place at this time.

Within another month, a friend phoned and asked me whether I knew that my husband had made arrangements to move into their home! I took the call at work with my boss standing in front of me. I don't know what I looked like, but I felt the blood drain out of me. I just dried up, and I could barely speak, but I attempted to maintain a professional exterior. I thanked the friend for the call, asked my boss if I could leave for the day saying, 'I've just been told my husband is leaving me and I need to go home'. I got ready and as I left I said 'how do you get through this?' and walked in a daze to my car. As I drove out of the complex and turned onto the main road all I could hear was this noise from the car and I wondered what it was until I realised – it was me!

I didn't know what I was doing, so, when all else fails, phone a friend. I called one of my sisters and unsuccessfully tried to tell her what happened – 'Waaaaahhhhhh.....he's........waaaaaaaahhhhhhh......'. I drove to the school where she was working at the time. (I probably shouldn't have been driving but somehow I got there) The children were having their break and were excited when I arrived, shouting 'Hi Laura...' I laughed with them – maintaining the stiff upper lip. I walked through to the back room and collapsed on the floor. I sobbed as my sister and the girls who worked at the school came in and just hugged me. It was so surreal! After a couple of hours of talking, weeping, hugging and praying I felt I had to leave. I really needed to be alone.

I got in the car (again!) and decided to head for Largs (when all else fails, go to Largs). On route I had such an urge for a fag. I hadn't smoked in 14 years! I headed into town like some covert operative as I was certain people could tell that my husband was leaving me. I bought a packet of 10 cigarettes and a box of matches and literally ran back to the car before anyone could see me! I drove back up to a local view point. I somehow staggered out of my car and noticed there was a man sitting in his car nearby. Again, I walked like some secret agent trying to avoid detection, as I was convinced he, too, would know that my husband was leaving me — surely there was a big neon sign above me notifying the world I was losing my husband? I was broken.

It was the most beautiful day, Mediterranean blue sky, birds soaring, barely a cloud in the sky. I just sat there, tears streaming down my face, as I realised life carries on around you even when your world falls in! I just said, 'Oh God help me!' I tried to light the first cigarette but between the wind on the hill and my shaking it took about four matches! Finally, it was lit, and after chain smoking three fags, I laughed at myself and looked up to the heavens saying, 'God, now I remember why I quit'. As I sat there, unable to stop the tears from flowing, I felt God say, 'Laura, you cannot fall apart because he walks out of your life. Will you trust Me?'

I wanted to but I was so scared!

I was becoming more distressed so rather than 'lose it' on a hillside in Largs, I got back in the car and attempted to make it home. I made it as far as the first lay-by where I pulled in, vomited and sobbed myself to sleep…

What seemed like an eternity, but was only hours later, I drove home and parked a little way from the house. I wasn't sure if he would be there packing and I couldn't bear the thought of seeing that. Then I realised, he hadn't called me himself. He had told me nothing of his plans. He hadn't said he was leaving. I didn't even know if it was true!

I called him after getting myself together. He was so strong on the phone and I was broken. He came home later that night and we talked. He didn't leave.

From that day on I threw myself completely on God, and prayed that He would somehow work it all out and help me. I'd realised my husband had taken priority in my life, and somewhere along the line God had been relegated to second place. I just hadn't realised till that day.

What commenced was what I have called 'the journey', for it was not a quick turnaround, but a step by step, day by day, sometimes hour by hour walk with God; discovering His love for me which knows no bounds, His grace to bring me through, and His belief and faith in me to overcome whatever circumstances.

I discovered intimacy with God which I guard jealously now.

There were many things that God dealt with during this time; here are a few in summary:

Making Idols of relationships

Remembering to put God into first place for only He can tell you your true value and worth. Not believing the lie that your happiness depends upon another person or thing.

Taking responsibility

Not blaming others for everything that went wrong, even when they were at fault, but accepting my role in what happened.

Creating a haven of peace and love

Making a house a home where my husband would want to be. A place of peace and love away from the 'busy' world in which we live.

Loving unconditionally/being loving unconditionally

Learning to love, even when I was rejected, abused, and despite it all, loving all the more.

Standing firm

When all falls down around me, not throwing a 'wobbly' when God doesn't perform like 'Santa Claus', but, standing in the midst of the chaos, trusting in Him despite the circumstances.

During these times I wrote songs, many of which had the theme of intimacy in walking with God, talking with Him like Adam had in the beginning – daily, intimately, sharing openly, between two friends.

Those were very dark days yet somehow there was a strength that came on a daily basis which carried me through each day!

By August we had our first day out together in four months. We went cycling and had a little picnic in the morning. Later we went to Glasgow for some frames for my Dad's room, as I had been re-decorating it for him. We had returned home, and I was cutting the material for curtains for Dad's room. My husband came in and told me to sit down. I thought he was kidding around. After several attempts to get me to sit down he told me my Dad was dead! I had always been a person who was so strong, but the previous months had taken their toll, along with life just crushing me — I crumpled to the floor in a heap and silently screamed. I looked up at my husband's face and realised he was not going to handle my broken state so I got up and said, 'You have to take me to Dad's.' As we drove my husband said, 'It's always a disaster, the first day we have together and this...' I knew how he felt! I stayed with my Dad until the funeral staff came for him, and how I dealt with it is a whole other story in itself. I returned home hours later and just said, 'God, You've got to bring good out of this!'

My husband withdrew from me, and very difficult days followed, but in the midst of the difficulties, more songs poured forth from me.

God had begun to bring in a support structure. He literally told me to 'get a life'. I had spent most of my marriage waiting for my husband to come home, and we generally only went out as a couple. I would never have gone out alone — I was too scared. Since our move, I had barely been out and God showed me that this was not helping, with me being so isolated. He told me to make friends — I didn't know how. I just felt so unloved, so unwanted, so worthless, *WHO* would want to be my friend? I saw no good in myself so why would people want to be with me — my husband didn't want to be with me, and he was supposed to be my best friend. Despite this, I prayed that God would help me, give me some good friends, and help me not to be so scared of everything. I started going out with one of my sisters on a regular basis. I made some new friends, and I overcame my fear of going out alone. I went to my first ballet (it was so good I went to three of them within a month) and my first opera – amazing! By the spring of 2003, I even went away for a weekend on my own (I had originally booked for my husband and I but he wouldn't come with me so I went alone). God was doing a work in my life and changing me.

After nine months of permanent nightshift, with my husband and I barely seeing each other, my Dad's death and my partner's lack of support, plus my health deteriorating, at times I felt so desperately alone and fearful. The enemy would come with negative thoughts, as well as using circumstances, to convince me to give up and take the easy way out. I would pray in and around the house, reading encouraging scriptures out loud and try not to be afraid. Since Dad's death, I had started having panic attacks, and these became increasingly worse. I was so convinced, at these times, that I was going to die, yet in the midst of the horridness there were occasions when my husband astounded me with his understanding and love. However, these times were few and far between. I was on medication to help reduce and control the panic attacks, as they literally immobilised me, and then I injured my back. I was given two different types of tablets to help reduce the pain and help me get around. My back became increasingly worse and I returned to the doctor, who gave me another drug to try. I was to take it just before going to bed.

My sister was visiting and left in the early hours. I took the new tablet and fell into a deep sleep but not for long – I awoke with my heart pumping so rapidly it was coming out of my chest, my tongue was swelling, I had difficulty breathing and I knew this was not good! I felt such a horrid 'darkness' in the house and sensed I was in trouble. I dialled my sister's number, then my husband's number but there was no answer. By this point I was on my knees praying as I dialled 999. When the paramedics arrived I had gone into shock but as soon as I was coherent, I prayed that God would despatch His angels to protect me. I arrived at the hospital and they did whatever it is they do and attached me to a monitor. I continued to pray that God would help me — I suddenly had the urge to vomit. With a bed pan in hand I vomited until there was nothing left and lay back exhausted and shaken.

Meanwhile the hospital had been trying to contact my husband at work with no success. After a couple of hours in observation I was told I could go home. The hospital staff had finally managed to speak to my husband but were told he couldn't come and get me. The hospital arranged for a taxi and paid for it, the taxi driver made sure I got into the house. It had been a drug reaction, and I believe without a shadow of doubt that God protected me and preserved my life that night.

The situation at home just got worse. I felt I couldn't carry on, and was looking to leave. By December I had a mortgage arranged and was going to view a flat. When reading my Bible, I very clearly heard God said 'stay!' The scripture was Isaiah 52:12, 'you will not leave in a hurry, running for your lives. For the Lord will go ahead of you and the God of Israel will protect you from behind' (NLT). Nobody knew what was going on – at this point I still couldn't be honest with myself, never mind anyone else. I would have died before telling anyone these most private details of my life. I decided to trust God and I didn't leave.

At work my role changed. I was forced to do a job I didn't want to, and I was so fearful of saying no, Even when I did, it made no difference. Little did I know things there were going to get a whole lot worse! My ability to maintain perfection was diminishing fast; I was juggling balls, spinning plates, performing acrobatics and from the outside I appeared (apparently) calm, cool, collected, confident, and assured, when inside I was screaming 'stop the world; I want to get off!'

Every morning I had such a sense of dread, and I would cry out to God to give me the strength to get through each day — I did this almost every day for nearly 3 years. Frequently I would pray this prayer: 'God, I don't have the ability to overcome this, but I choose not to give in. Help me, Father!'

Shortly after, even though I had said nothing about my home situation to anyone, I was given a book called 'The power of a praying wife' written by Stormie O'Martian. Even reading the introduction, I was weeping, as this woman seemed to know exactly how I was feeling, and so I took to heart what she said. The next 'workshop with God' dealt with the following:

Forgiveness

Unconditionally and continually – my husband, friends, family, colleagues and myself.

Repentance (a few examples)

Judging – I had judged my parents, but the Bible tells us we are to honour them, I had brought 'curses' upon myself by judging them, and I had to forgive my wrong and their wrong.

Pride – the kind of pride I speak of is not the 'I'm great'/'I deserve better' type but the kind, 'I have fought to get to where I am'.

False humility – putting myself down in the hope that others would boost my low 'morale'.

Failing to trust God; to believe God's evaluation of my life; to see the meaning/purpose for my life.

Self righteous – 'I'm no good but I'm not that bad'!

Overcoming fears

Fear of showing weakness/lack of strength - this caused me to be uptight and controlled.

Fear of failure – you name it, I felt it.

Fear of the unknown – I couldn't face a day without knowing what it held; in my mind I would work out every possible scenario of what could go wrong, and would even have a back-up for my back-up plans.

Fear of man and rejection - this caused me to compromise, to compare myself to others and conform to their expectations in order to be loved and accepted.

Areas I was 'delivered'/'released'/'healed' from were: suicide, death, disappointment, failure, negativity, self-pity, despair, hopelessness, perfectionism, false responsibility, insecurity. No self esteem and no self-worth had built in me negative thought patterns and mindsets based on past experiences, which were causing me to consider reverting to old addictions, habits, destructive relationships.

Learning to say no
Losing my red cape!

I learned instead that I am loved. God is not waiting to beat me, He's not angry because of 'blocked channels' in my life, He's ready to help me. I am not a disappointment to Him. He's not wanting to clone me, He's made me to be me – unique and His!

I learned that hell is not just flames of fire but separation from God.

I dared to hope!

By July 2004 I was shocked to realise I was not really a teenager any more. I was an adult and it was time to accept this gracefully. Married life had settled out a bit, and we were getting on better. The following month we even talked and agreed to start a family in the New Year. The house conversion was all but complete, our home was looking good – a building site no more! I'd even had a 'Virgin Vie' party with my family and friends and I realised how lucky I was and how much I had changed. All these people around me! I could finally see God bringing about all I had desired and hoped for, to be a good friend, a loving wife and a future mom!

And yet, there was so much *angst* in me. Although I had accepted my husband might never return to 'walk with God' as he had before, I missed his 'fellowship' at church and I felt God had not finished His 'excavation' in my life.

By September, despite improved circumstances, I believed I was losing my mind and I couldn't keep it together any longer. I was exhausted physically, mentally, emotionally and spiritually. My husband and I went for a break away to see my family; it was there my aunt took me out for a walk and a talk! I surprised myself by opening up about so much that was going on in my life with work, church, home and I wept so much that day as we walked. It was time for me to lay down some of my busy schedule, to prioritise and learn to say 'no'. I popped into a wee chemist shop which had a book section and I was drawn to this particular book. As I drew it off the shelf I saw it was by Stormie O'Martian (the same author of 'Power of a praying wife'), entitled 'Lord, I want to be whole'. I had a quick glance at the content. It seemed to be everything God was showing me, but I just wasn't ready for it. I left it on the shelf and came home. Within no time at all, I started to see how I should 'let things go'. A friend came, shortly after that trip, and said she had been in a bookshop in Glasgow; this book literally leapt off the shelf — no prizes for guessing what the book was!

I started to read it, and prayed about each area as I read, asking God to show me clearly what specifically related to me. One particular area was negative ties — unhealthy relational or negative attachments; it could be people or things and I felt God was telling me to 'clear out' — this was confirmed through a friend, who had been praying for me and had the same message.

Here I was at home, as I had a couple of days leave. I decided it was probably time to go through Dad's things. After his death I just couldn't throw anything away, so I had 'bagged' and 'boxed' the majority of his belongings - tapes,videos,etc. - and put it all in my loft. Between this and the boxes of 'stuff' I'd kept and carried from house to house, never reading, never using — I felt it was time for it all to go!

I had not run from Dad's death, but faced it, felt it and let the grief work its course through me — and it was time to let go. During this 'clear out' I discovered a couple of letters which astounded me. One was from my Gran, who I thought utterly hated me. From the content, I realised she actually loved me! Another was from a girl I had known years ago; from her letter I realised she had regarded me as a friend. I had never felt that way, I had always felt unloved, unwanted, a failure, a disappointment and I couldn't believe anyone would value me. Sadly, my Gran had died, so I couldn't talk to her, but I made my peace with her that day, and I also wrote to the girl.

By the time I had finished, I had taken two car loads of stuff to the thrift shop, three loads to the dump and still had 20-30 black bags of rubbish in the kitchen. When I saw it all there, the thought hit me 'you've carried all this stuff around with you for years' – no wonder I was exhausted! After I cleared it, I felt lighter and slightly exhilarated. I didn't stop there. I had some difficult decisions to make, and felt that my life depended upon me doing them. During October/November I resigned from the 'hell' job and stood up for myself for the first time in my life. I also stepped down from all activities and roles within the church.

Suddenly, although I knew it was right to do all these things and step back, I didn't know who I was; I felt like I was free-falling with the weight of a grand piano and the speed of a bullet, and it wasn't a pleasant experience! My worth and my identity had been tied up in my job, my service, my living up to everyone's expectations – I had just resigned from it all and I was lost! There were people who didn't understand my stepping back, but supported me anyway, and there were those who just didn't understand. For me, God had to show me that it was ok to do *nothing*, He would still love me, my identity was not in any of these things and I had to discover who I was in Him!

I was becoming undone! My 'safe' had been cracked. I was finally admitting to people I was broken. During this time an area I faced was the death of my Mum. She had died when I was 12, and I had never dealt with it, or allowed the grief to come. Don't get me wrong, I wept every single year for 22 years, around the time of her death, but I had never faced the fact she was gone. I never said goodbye, and this had affected so much of my life and how I dealt with things. I realised I had to let her go. Surrounded by friends, I sobbed as I saw her in my mind's eye, and I cried out 'I don't want her to go'. The child in me was still there, holding on even after 22 years. Goodbye was not a word I had ever used, I always said 'see you later' – that night I finally let her go and said goodbye.

A friend gave me a scripture verse which said 'now is the time of God's favour'. I encouraged myself that things would get better. Within the week I had my first car accident! I took a bend on a country road; I am not entirely sure what happened, but the car spun out of control, like a spinning top, for a few hundred yards. I knew if anyone came round the approaching bend we'd both be dead. Somehow I managed to slow the car and ended in a ditch backwards. As the car halted on the fence, several cars came round the bend. I had been protected but immediately a wee voice said, 'Oh yeah, time of God's favour?' and I immediately replied, 'I'm alive, amn't I!'

The car had the smallest scratch, but I was shaken and unharmed. The thing was, I hadn't wanted to go out, but my husband insisted that I meet him at my sister's as he was doing a job there. Now I was going to have to tell him that his car was in a ditch. He was not happy! He didn't care that I hadn't been injured. I realised that night that I wasn't loved and yet I still had to love him! The verse 'no weapon forged against you will prevail' became very real to me – there had been a few incidents prior and this was another – God was keeping His word on a regular basis!

God spoke to me again. There was to be no straddling the fence, I had to take a stand and refuse to let the enemy steal faith, hope and love from me. I was to face the fire and — despite the circumstances and past experiences — believe! How hard I found this, as my circumstances were dire.

During this time I heard a 'sermon' by an American preacher, Bishop TD Jakes, on amazing grace and I was encouraged by what he said. *"Grace cannot be seen in perfect situations, but works in imperfect and uncomfortable situations. There are circumstances that don't change so that God can take us through. He won't change it so we can see His grace. He'll help us get through some things that should kill us but we will see His grace. You may feel like you're going to lose your mind but He won't let you lose your mind and when it's all over you're going to see and say 'amazing grace'!"*

My reliance could no longer be on myself, for my ability to 'fight' my way to survival had diminished. Circumstances were so overwhelming; within me I felt a darkness growing and coming my way that I couldn't explain.

A friend encouraged me by saying that there couldn't possibly be more as I'd been stripped back to nothing. She said that out of it all would come an amazing story – she was right about the story but I don't think any of us could have imagined what came next...

At New Year my husband and I went away for a week. I realised during that time he was 'running away'; he told me it was all in my imagination. In my heart I decided to pray fervently for his return to God as I could not go through what we'd been through again. That Thursday we drove home; it was really tense. By the time we were in the house he just told me 'no children – no way, no how' and then asked if I was going to leave him. I was broken. We went to bed, only I lay there screaming silently.

In my mind I walked before the throne of God. With a knife, I cut my chest open and my heart fell forward 'is this what you want?' Then I walked up to the throne and I laid down a baton. I turned, mumbling 'I've failed you and I cannot do what you ask...I've failed..I've failed...'

Walking away I heard God say my name,

'Laura'

I kept walking..

'*Laura*'..

I turned and God was there, He just held me and I began to sob like I'd never sobbed.

For the first time in our marriage I did not shield my husband from my pain. The next morning I brought out the little baby-gro; this was how I had been going to tell him when I became pregnant. I had even bought maternity wear in anticipation of us starting a family. I was angry; he'd lied and led me to believe, again, and my insides felt shredded. We tried to have a nice day together, but it felt so farcical. That night, for the first time in our nine years of marriage, I could not lie down beside him. I had to speak to God. I went downstairs and just cried to God to help me. I wanted to leave and in my head I was planning my departure. My husband came down and stood naked before me and said 'Please don't throw us away, don't go'. As I looked at him, I knew I couldn't hurt him, I loved him so much and, even with this pain, I could never hurt him.

I needed time alone and said as such, as gently as I could, to give me some time. I said I'd be up, but I couldn't conceal my pain. I lay there and God told me to stay, to go back upstairs and sleep beside him and to trust that God would work it out. Hope arose – God could still sort it! I went back up and lay beside him and as he came out of his sleep and he realised I was there, he breathed a sigh of relief and went back to sleep. I was glad I was still on holiday!

The next day, while my husband was at work I got on my knees and prayed, I laid my desire for a baby in God's hands, as I felt there was a battle coming, and you can't fight when your hands are full. The things God had taught me, to love, to create a haven of peace and love etc, came back to me, so I went out and bought a dining suite and changed the baby's room into a dining room. I prayed over it and made a special meal for two and I truly believed God would work things out. We had a meal together, but my husband had to go out to a job that night.

Five days later he told me he wanted to get a vasectomy, asking if I was going to leave him. Again I was taken aback, even jokingly commented, 'Are you trying to get rid of me…what's the rush? You got some young chick lined up to move in here?…'

I had been praying fervently for 10 days, that God would do a miracle, praying very specific prayers for his life, and that what was done in secret would be revealed…

On Saturday night, my husband called to say he'd have to go to another emergency job. I was praying and felt God told me to check his mobile phone! *NEVER* had I done such a thing, it showed such distrust. But I said if that's what I was to do, then God would need to make it possible, as this man and his phone were rarely apart. In addition, there was my regular morning hibernation status.

God made sure I was awake first thing on the Sunday morning — through my husband, as he got up, knocking everything over by his bedside and me having stomach cramps. I went to get a hot water bottle, my heart racing, for there, lying beside the kettle, was his phone…

Psalm 55 says:

'Listen to my prayer O God; do not ignore my cry for help.

Please listen and answer me for I am overwhelmed by my troubles. My enemies shout at me, making loud and wicked threats. They bring trouble on me hunting me down in their anger. My heart is in anguish. The terror of death overpowers me. Fear and trembling overwhelm me, I can't stop shaking.

Oh how I wish I had wings like a dove, then I would fly away and rest. I would fly far away to the quiet of the wilderness.

How quickly I would escape – far away from this wild storm of hatred. I see violence and strife in the city. It's walls are patrolled day and night against invaders, but the real danger is wickedness within the city. Murder and robbery are everywhere there; threats and cheating are rampant in the streets.

It is not an enemy who taunts me – I could bear that. It is not my foes who so arrogantly insult me – I could have hidden from them. Instead it is you, my equal, my companion and close friend. What good fellowship we enjoyed as we walked to the house of God...but I will call on God and the Lord will rescue me.

Morning, noon and night I plead aloud in my distress, and the Lord hears my voice. He rescues me and keeps me safe from the battle waged against me, even though many still oppose me. God who is King forever will hear me and will humble them. For my enemies refuse to change their ways, they do not fear God. As for this friend of mine, he betrayed me; he broke his promises, His words are as smooth as cream but in his heart is war. His words are as soothing as lotion but underneath are daggers. Give your burdens to the Lord and He will take care of you. He will not permit the godly to slip and fall...but I am trusting you to save me...' (NLT).

Revelation and Restoration

I stood, shaking, my heart racing, wondering whether I should hide what I now knew, but God hadn't brought me this far to turn back. I forwarded to my mobile the message that I read, and wondered who it was that my husband had become so close to that 'guilt', 'divorce' and 'affair' were mentioned in her message to him.

It was no longer a time to hide but a time to confront, so I did. I walked upstairs, adrenaline coursing through me, to our bathroom where he was showering. I pulled back the shower curtain and showed him his phone. (He must have thought I was going to re-create a scene from 'Psycho'!) I didn't say anything but his face confirmed my worse fears. The colour drained from his face. When I stated 'I've been right all along – haven't I?' I was filled with such a deep sense of sadness, for what I had hoped I had been wrong to question.

Suddenly so many things fell into place. His treatment of me; his pushing of me all the time, as if he wanted me to go. Those hypothetical questions about us separating and who would get the house. Now it all made sense. With this in mind, I told him I had not worked as hard as I had, creating a home where I had expected our children to be, to have someone else move in with him – the house would be sold before I watched that happen.

He said many things, but it was mostly panic speaking. He'd been found out, and was trying to talk his way out of it, and he still wasn't being honest. To this day I don't know the entire truth, but I don't need to know. God revealed just enough for the truth to be seen.

My husband left that morning in a panic, heading for work, refusing to take time off, even for this. I didn't know what to do, it all felt so surreal. I wanted to believe our marriage was not over. I believed God could work a miracle, but for that to happen we *both* had to want it.

I sat on the edge of my bed and looked in the mirror, which I rarely did as I felt so ugly, so fat, so useless and as I looked at my reflection, this day was no different - the feelings of contempt arose as I glared at my reflection, 'I hate you, look at you, no wonder your husband is leaving!'

I got up and staggered downstairs, in shock and my mind spinning. I lifted the phone and called one of my sisters, only managing to say 'He's been having an affair. Help me please', before I broke down.

Waiting for her to arrive, I didn't know what to do. I wept, and my mind ran wild with many different scenarios of what could be, but a part of me felt such relief – *I wasn't losing my mind!* Until this point I believed I was going insane. Three years of extreme stress and pressure from all areas of my life had broken me.

So I prayed!

You see, I always believed the best of him, even when faced with the hard facts. I believed in him because God had taught me to love — to truly love, without conditions, without cause, just to love, holding no resentment, holding no unforgiveness, to love as if I had never been hurt. And even now, I loved him, knowing the worst of him, I loved him.

I called his parents. Their (lack of) reaction surprised me, and I think they had somehow known. I emailed his manager, for his relationship with one of his employees was forbidden, and I was concerned for her welfare. It was strange that I felt no anger, no rage toward either of them. In days of old I would have retaliated by hunting her down and castrating him, but here I was in a place of ultimate betrayal, and I found myself praying for them both! This is how I know God is real and His hand in my life had changed me so much!

I barely remember my sister arriving. I just remember my heart was being ripped apart and I clung to the carpet with my fingernails for fear that I would fall off this earth. The pain in my chest was a physical pain which surprised me, it was not a metaphorical turn of phrase; my heart was ripping apart and that pain remained for many months.

As my sister held me, a rollercoaster of emotions surged through me. I felt so ashamed – I never wanted to leave the house again, I didn't want anyone to know. What was I to do? We prayed! She called one of my other sisters and my best friend, and soon the four of us together prayed that God would work out the whole situation.

I was so afraid. I feared for my husband; I saw this as a crucial time and the decision he made now would affect our lives and the lives of many others.

In the midst of all these powerful, overwhelming emotions I felt a strange calm come over me.

By mid afternoon on that first day I asked the girls to pray for me, that I would not be blinded but would have such wisdom to know what to do. I felt I had to 'hand over' the whole situation to God and trust that

He would work it out for my best – *whatever* the outcome. I found it difficult to pray initially as I didn't truly want the 'whatever' outcome. I wanted to be married, have my husband back, have our family, see my dreams come true. I laid it all aside and eventually managed to make the decision to trust God, for, whatever the outcome — and as difficult and overwhelming as the whole thing was — I wanted to make a 'symbolic' gesture. I had a clay figure of a couple, which I had felt represented us as husband and wife, so I decided, afraid as I was, I would burn this. Full of emotion, while the other three looked on. I sat on the floor as I took the figure and started a fire in the wood burner. Once it was going I placed the figure in. It was very emotional; I was weeping, and felt something of a 'hold' was broken by this gesture. I watched as the figure lay there in the midst of the flames; what had started as a serious act became quite comical. The figure wouldn't catch alight! My weeping ceased as I focused on keeping the fire lit, I put some more newspapers in around to help encourage it on – still to no avail. By this point we were all laughing as I put some vegetable fat on it to aid the ignition – this did the trick! The solemnity of the situation had been lifted and I was glad. My sense of humour remained in the midst of shattered hopes and dreams!

My friend read this verse in Psalm 42 which seemed to cry out everything I was feeling right there and then:

"As the deer pants for streams of water, so I long for you O God. I thirst for God, the living God. When can I come and stand before Him? Day and night I have only tears for food while my enemies continually taunt me saying, 'where is this God of yours?' My heart is breaking as I remember how it used to be; I walked among the crowds of worshippers, leading a great procession to the house of God, singing for joy and giving thanks – it was the sound of a great celebration! Why am I so discouraged? Why so sad? I will put my hope in God! I will praise Him again – my Saviour and my God! Now I am deeply discouraged but I will remember your kindness. I hear the tumult of the raging seas as your waves and surging tides sweep over me. Through each day the Lord pours His unfailing love upon me and through each night I sing His songs, praying to God who gives me life. 'O God my rock' I cry, 'why have you forsaken me? Why must I wander in darkness oppressed by my enemies? Their

taunts pierce me like a fatal wound, they scoff 'where is this God of yours?' Why am I so discouraged? Why so sad? I will put my hope in God! I will praise Him again – my Saviour and my God"

My husband came home after his shift. The girls had left me alone for a few hours to allow us to talk. I had asked him in the morning to find somewhere to stay for the next couple of weeks. I wanted him to take time alone to decide what he wanted. Did he want the marriage? Did he want to be free? I felt he had to do this alone so he could make the decision un-influenced by me or anyone else. I told him I loved him and if he wanted the marriage then we could work through things. I didn't want him to stay because he felt he had to, or it was the right thing to do, or because he didn't want to lose out materially. I only wanted him to stay if he loved me and really wanted to stay. He left that night, taking his clothes and promising to call.

As he walked out the door, I locked it behind him and returned to the lounge, where I collapsed on the floor and sobbed. I saw my hopes and dreams walk out with him. Ever since I'd met him I'd loved him with such a passion. I wanted to have his children, not just any child, his child. I loved everything about him; his hands, his fingers, his feet, his toes, his stomach and the way the hair grew on it, the scent of him, not an aftershave or body spray but him. I wanted to grow old loving him and him loving me – but these vanished with him at that moment.

I cried out to God, silent screams filled my being and I could contain it no more. A deep mournful wail escaped and I sobbed on the floor. Worship music had been playing in the background and as I lay there it seemed to surround me. I felt God surrounding me and I was overwhelmed by the love I felt. A peace and calm came over me and comforted me. The sobbing ceased and I stood to my feet, I raised my arms, as a child to its Father, and in that moment I know I was held by the King of Heaven.

Questions arose. 'Who am I?', 'What do I do now? 'My life is over!' Above the clamour God spoke, 'My child, you are mine! Your life is not over! Trust Me; I will work all things out for your good!' So I took God at His word.

My sisters and friend worked like a tag-team that first week, taking turns to stay over at night. They were amazing; I have been truly blessed out of my socks by my family and friends!

After four days I had heard nothing from my husband, other than he had found a place to stay temporarily. I called him and was told he didn't know what he was going to do, he was busy, his mind a jumble, he couldn't decide. I asked him one question - 'Have you seen her?' His reply was yes. So I said you've made your decision then – he said nothing and our call ended. I decided then to get a solicitor. Later that day and the following I received text messages from his relatives expressing how sorry they were to hear. 'Hear what?' I asked. My husband had told me nothing, but he had told his family our marriage was over!!

That weekend, although he had been staying in another area, he visited our local cinema with his girlfriend. There were many friends there, for the early and later evening shows, who saw them together. I was so ashamed and embarrassed, while both one of my sisters and I received concerned calls that weekend.

From day one of him leaving, I felt I had to fast and pray, regarding the whole situation but especially for my husband. On the tenth day I had to write a letter which I believe was God's heart toward him. After finishing it, my fast ended.

I now had to be strong when I really didn't feel it!

I arranged to see a solicitor and in that second week my husband and I met to discuss the separation agreement. I had prayed we would both be able to do this reasonably and fairly. As it happened, it was the best talk we had and was so surreal – he told me how he loved me 'but just not as his wife'. How he hadn't been honest when we met and how now he just wanted to be free. We spoke at length - we even laughed! It was the last time.

During the meeting we agreed to split the proceeds of the house and belongings 50/50 and a list was drawn up. He was in a hurry and wanted the money from the house sale soon, but I was in no position to move and the house was in no state to be sold, so we agreed if I could get a mortgage I would buy him out. He wanted to move quickly and sought a divorce. I felt it was all too quick and said so, but we agreed that if after two years we were still apart, we would not hold one another to the marriage. It was written into the separation agreement that both parties would agree to divorce after two years.

He had bought an Audi and I didn't want it. We had a Morris Minor, which I drove at the time, but mileage restrictions on the insurance meant it had to be sold. He also had an old van which he gave me but, owing to my back problems, and the lack of power steering, it was too heavy and painful to drive so it too was sold. I received £1200 from the sale of these two vehicles but had to find a replacement car soon.

At subsequent meetings I found him unreasonable. He would later call and apologise for the way he had treated me but his manner didn't change. There were a couple of calls, after he moved away, where I found him difficult, so I make the decision to cease all contact, as it was breaking me each time.

I have to share this as it truly was a miracle. You may say it was coincidence, but for me it was God letting me know He was looking out for me.

My search for another car was so stressful. I knew very little about them and my limited budget didn't help. I enrolled the help of one of my sisters, who drove me round every garage and second hand dealership in a 50 mile radius for two days. And I was assisted by a gem of a bloke at the garage where I had my car repaired - he must have taken twenty calls a day, trying to advise me, telling me what to look for. Between this and the *Auto Trader* I was sure I would find something, but no. I came home on the second night of the search and screamed. I found it all so frustrating! That night I prayed, 'God, I quite like Ford Kas, racing green is a real nice colour, not too old with a reasonable mileage and no more than £1500 - please help me.' I had a meeting with the solicitor the next morning but, before leaving the house, I felt God saying 'check the *Auto Trader*'. I was in a rush as I had a bus to catch and local public transport was limited but the feeling persisted. I quickly dialled up the internet and checked the *Auto Trader* and guess what was there – a racing green Ford Ka, P reg, 63K on the clock, and on sale for £1500.

I printed off the information, stuffed it in my bag and ran for the bus. When I left the solicitors, I was a bit emotional, and had forgotten about the car. I had gone right round the block before I realised I had walked in a circle. Then the thought of the 'Ka' came to me, I pulled out the piece of paper, not feeling very hopeful, and dialled the number. It was a dealership in Glasgow and the car was there and available for a test drive. My next quandary was, how could I get there? My mobile rang in my hand. It was one of my sisters asking me what I was doing! We headed for Glasgow, and within an hour of arriving I drove away with my racing green ford Ka – thanking God because He heard me and He didn't miss a single detail! Even now when I'm driving it, I remember that day and smile.

During this time I continued to pray that God would guide me, giving me the strength and wisdom to make the right decisions. I also prayed that I would learn all I could from this – about myself, about others. From the very first day God started to show me, He challenged me to face the facts about the nature of my marital relationship, and revealed truth. When I looked at the last few years, I was overwhelmed by the victim I had become, because of the low opinion I had of myself, and the wrong values/evaluation of who I was. I had compromised in so many areas, in an attempt to hold on, but with hindsight I see God had been working from the top down; my work, church, friends, relationships, now my marriage and to me. All that was wrong was removed, restored and in many ways, I have been rebuilt.

Up until my husband's return to his family I believed there was still hope of reconciliation, but when I realised he was taking this girl with him, I knew it was over for me. The picture I had at the time, if I did not proceed with the divorce, was that it would be like having a corpse tied to me. So when my husband informed me of his imminent return to his parents' home, I said I would be filing for divorce. His reaction threw me, for this had been what he was 'pushing' for, yet initially he refused. After some thought, I realised that this was my decision too, and his refusal could not stop it. I spoke to the solicitor and proceeded with the action on the grounds of adultery. My husband then agreed to co-operate. To save going through courts, he provided a statement acknowledging his adultery and his father confirmed that this girl was living under his roof with my husband. Divorce was such a difficult decision to make and I struggled so with it – I couldn't believe this was happening. I felt I had betrayed myself for I was unable to keep my vow to stand by his side until death parted us. God showed me that it was the right thing to do, and that I had to continue to trust that He knew best. I thank God for surrounding me with people who did not judge but supported me throughout!

The day after I found out about my husband's unfaithfulness, this was the daily reading in the 'Word for Today': -

"God is capable of handling anything you bring to Him. Creating planets is no problem for Him; neither is taking the little you have

and making it go a long way. Nothing is too difficult for Him; He is just waiting for you to recognise that."

(excerpt from 'The Word for Today' - see reference page)
The following day it was: -

"A sense of value – Adam had a relationship with God before he had one with Eve. Why? Because nobody but God can tell you who you are and what you're worth. Until you know that you will not know whether you are in love or in need. You will keep looking for somebody to love you so much that you will finally start feeling good about yourself. The trouble is, when you find that person, you will cling to them like a vine. You will agree with all their opinions and have none of your own. You will try to meet their every need and make yourself indispensable and you will feel threatened if they can do anything without you. When they enjoy someone else's' company you'll panic and say 'all I need is you, how come you don't feel the same way?' No human relationship can sustain such a load. Adam learned to relate to Eve only after he had learned to relate to God. It is in God's presence, free from the demands of others that you begin to look at yourself in the right mirror. It is there you prepare the gift to be given. But something has changed, now you know how much the gift is worth and you will give it only to someone who places the same value on it. God has always wanted the best for you; He's just waiting for you to come into agreement with Him. Isaiah 44:2 'I am your Creator; you were in my care even before you were born.' "

(excerpt from 'The Word for Today' - see reference page)
My husband had not been honest when we met; during our meeting, he told me he had agreed with all I said I liked, and just went along with everything, so I would marry him! I realised we both had such deep needs when we met, and I asked God to reveal to me areas in my life that needed to be set right. Another deeper journey had begun for me.

God gave me one day in June 2005 — a pre-taster of what my future life would be — I was flying. I didn't think it possible to feel so free, so light and I realised I had never in my life experienced it and I wanted that. I was standing in my office and I danced in a circle, like my pottery angel — I was free to sing, to dance, to laugh, to create.

Isaiah 40:25-31 says,

'To whom will you compare Me? Who is my equal? asks the Holy One. Look up into the heavens. Who created all the stars? He brings them out one after another, calling each by its name. And He counts them to see that none are lost or have strayed away. How can you say the Lord does not see your troubles? How can you say God refuses to hear your case? Have you never heard or understood? Don't you know that the Lord is the everlasting God, the Creator of all the earth? He never grows faint or weary. No one can measure the depths of His understanding. He gives power to those who are tired and worn out; He offers strength to the weak. Even youths will become exhausted, and young men will give up. But those who wait on the Lord will find new strength. They will fly high on wings like eagles. They will run and not grow weary. They will walk and not faint.' (NLT).

I am a miracle; I am a testimony of God's love, comfort, grace and strength. My valley of trouble has indeed become a gateway of hope - free from worry/anxiety!

God encouraged me to keep on going.

Don't let previous happenings shade your tomorrow. God is the God of second chances. When your outlook is bleak and you have tried everything and nothing's working, and you are ready to give up because you have a pile of past disappointments keeping your dreams buried. God knows how hard you have worked; He sees your discouragement and He invites you to try again but with Him this time.

I had such deep insecurity, and a battleground in my mind, and the need to work things out. I found it impossible to function on a daily basis without feeling secure in 'knowing' what I was doing (I discovered this had started when my mum died, and I had been taken completely unawares – I never wanted to be so unprepared again).

I had to be realistic and responsible, acknowledging what was happening; the loss, the grief, the pain, the lies and deceit for so long. I had to maintain the support mechanisms that had been put in place, despite how I felt, to face life with optimism, lighten my load, throwing 'baggage overboard' and drawing into God.

I realised that God wants me to have life and life abundantly — spiritually, emotionally, physically, mentally — the full package!

I didn't want to rush into any other relationship, as hard as this is, for there are times you just want to be held, to be loved, to have someone there. I fought the desire, especially in the early days, as I'd always felt loved when 'I made love' but I knew that there is so much more. I wanted to learn and work through the good and the bad about myself. I've never been one for self-help books but a particular book which helped me tremendously was 'Growing through divorce' by Jim Smoke. I had thought ours was a good marriage, because we had a great sex life and rarely argued. That's not it! It's about loving one another despite it all. It's not about having 'power' or abusing someone's openness but wanting that person to be all they can be, loving them not because they 'do' for you but just loving them.

I returned to work in February, after four weeks off in which the separation was agreed, the financial wheels were set in motion and I had another car — the emotional jungle was what remained. Again God blew me away. With daily hugs from close work colleagues; their love and support was outstanding during that first year. I shared an office with one other person and we laughed so much together; cried together and she gave fantastic hugs! I am so blessed to have had these supportive people around me.

I discovered two of my close work 'pals' had also been divorced and I'd known nothing; they helped me so much.

One of my 'pals' emailed me daily and kept me supplied with DVDs and I watched every episode of *Stargate* from season 1-7, followed by *Starsky & Hutch*, season 1&2! Another 'pal' would give me sanity breaks in his office or a couple of us would go out for lunch or a drive when I felt the walls closing in.

I was glad to be occupied as it consumed my mind and I had a focus, but eventually it became too much. After almost a year in this post, I reached a place where I could be honest. I hated the job. I had only taken it because I felt I had to and I couldn't say no, but I'd now reached a place where I was so miserable I had to do something. My decision didn't go down well but I knew I had to get out/move on.

I made myself simple targets like:
   * Get up each morning.
   * Take a day at a time and if that was too much, try an hour or a
      minute at a time.

* Spend time with God each morning, having a quiet start to the day.
* Eating – even if I had no appetite, I'd eat fruit and at least one meal and take vitamin supplements to help.
* Resting – there is a risk to 'keeping busy' and I tried to have a healthy balance between staying in and going out activities.
* Ask for help.
* Let your emotions out – cry, scream (this should be done in a soundproof area or inside the car is good).
* Find out what I enjoyed and deciding what did I want to do?

The last one was particularly difficult for me as it seemed so selfish and the concept was foreign to me. I had lived my life trying to be what others wanted. and meeting their needs over my own. What I wanted didn't matter; it was time for my thinking to change!

I chose to take time out, visit the beach, head to Largs, travel North to see my family. I decided to take on nothing new, and make new friends. Most of all I chose to cut myself some slack! I have tried not to allow change to paralyse me! (I used to have such a sense of adventure in my late teens, always trying things, but somewhere along the line I'd lost it all, I let it all close in and got stuck in a comfort zone rut!)

I would continue to love and try to be fair.

God kept me when all I wanted to do was sell up and run away where no–one could see me. I have faced financial difficulties with bills beyond what I could manage but God told me to sit and rest and let things settle out before making ANY decisions. Thank God, He got me through it all!

I've come to realise God does not work the way I think He's going to. I had Him in a religious box of imagining how He should do things. Instead He blew me away. He is a God of the miraculous!

Take my divorce, in those first few days/months I just thought my life was over and yet I had such a sense that God could do anything. The whole process went so smoothly; even my solicitor acknowledged the miraculous in the speed of the separation and divorce settlement.

Take my hopes for a new love. I had my doubts! On one particular night I was overwhelmed that it would be impossible for me to find a man (no offence) who was the right age – I felt so old, ugly, worn and thought my chances of getting a 'decent' guy were slim. The TV was on but I wasn't really watching. As I sat on the couch considering my dim future before me when I looked at the screen and there was George Clooney!! *(One fine day)* Well, I just sat there, and the next thing I felt God saying – 'Look, Laura, there is hope!' —I burst out laughing — he must have been in his 40s when he made that movie! The following week I put a picture of George on my office wall, with, written above it, THERE IS HOPE just to remind me. Soon after, my 'best pal' and I were sitting one night. I was low. She said 'Heh, there's a great guy out there for you..' At that time it really was the last thing on my mind, and said as such, then looked at her and jokingly said 'although if it were the Scottish beef guy I might reconsider!' We laughed, and it became a wee joke. One day she phoned and said 'You're never gonna believe who's here!' The Scottish beef guy was filming in the village hall next door to the church. I had arranged to be off work, as my younger sister was returning from her round-the-world trip, and I was going to be about if she wanted. I was heading to the church on the Friday (last day of filming) and thinking about the SB guy being at Elderslie, and wondering what on earth caused them to film there of all places, and I felt God saying 'Laura – anything is possible!'. The following week, a picture of the Scottish beef guy was on my office wall with the words written above it 'ANYTHING IS POSSIBLE'

Not that God's going to get me the Scottish beef guy but it made me realise anything is possible!

After many broken months, with very rare 'good' days, I came home from church one day and just sobbed. I shouted out to God how I hated feeling this way, why was nothing changing, I still felt the agony, I still felt the rawness, I cried all the time, I couldn't sleep unless packed in pillows, I was tired of 'battling' the black hole that threatened to suck me into its vacuum. I sat on the edge of my bed and looked in the mirror, I waited for the hatred to rise as it usually did – it didn't come; instead I felt completely at peace. For the first time since I could remember I looked in the mirror and I no longer hated myself. I wept with joy! The work God was doing was so deep within, I wanted outward results and fast, He was working deep and taking the time He needed.

There were many 'firsts' that I faced.

On my first anniversary without him – such was the grace of God that day, I felt so thankful that I had known love and I could say that day, 'better to have loved and lost than to have never loved at all'!

One I have to share in particular was Christmas. I had made no firm plans with my family, but wanted to see how I was going to be on the day. We had our usual amazing candle-lit watchnight service at the church, and I was home late. I had fancied getting up on Christmas morning and going for a run on the beach; as it happened I slept late. Normally Christmas was like a military operation, but this year I just relaxed completely. There were no expectations! I got up wearing an oversized work t-shirt with my hair in that unique 'slept in' look and my eyes still in orbit. I couldn't find my slippers anywhere, so I gave up looking, wandered barefoot down to the kitchen, put on the coffee perc, switched on the oven for croissants and then put the heating on. It was a beautiful morning and I felt so at peace. The kitchen floor was quite cool and I couldn't be bothered going back upstairs and I saw my wellies (aqua paisley patterned) and thought why not?! I went through to the lounge and put on some 'rock' Christmas carols and danced round the living room, and thought my heart would burst with joy! The telephone rang; my sister checking that I was ok and would be going to her house for lunch. She asked if I'd opened my presents and what I was doing — as I told her that I was dancing round the living room in my big t-shirt and welly boots we both laughed. I hadn't realised the time, so I told her I would be late over. I sat down to open my presents. As I unwrapped them one at a time, I wept as I realised each person had thought of me, and each gift was beautiful. There was no disappointment overshadowing events as there had been in previous years when my husband had not bought me anything'

Once ready, I headed up to my sister's house. I realised I had not spent Christmas day with my family in 10 years. We all sat round the table and we could all feel it, we were together! We thanked God! We had a beautiful day and later I fell asleep in the chair whilst they watched my Christmas DVD 'Batman Returns' and it was the best time ever!

In the late summer, just the week my divorce came through, God brought someone into my life, for a season, just to give me a glimpse of what is possible with Him. It was amazing. I was drawn to this person and was like a 'guppy teenager' and I had never been like this before! We shared many similar interests. We had a love of music, dancing, walking, outdoors, leisure activities. It was an amazing time for me as I could be myself in all that I was. It didn't matter what I wore, or how high my shoes were, or how I wore my hair or what perfume I wore – this person accepted me as I was. We could talk round the clock (which we did frequently). After ten days with this man, I realised that in my marriage I had very little by comparison – this was a whole new experience for me in relationships. I felt I mattered and I felt totally and utterly loved. It was almost dream-like, his interest, his openness, I was thrilled!

We shared walks in the rain, up hills, barefoot on the beach, we'd sing together, play guitar together, dance together, laugh together, and cry together. He'd make me dinner; have lunchtime rendezvous, talk on the phone all night.

I also knew there were things that weren't quite right and as much as I wanted to ignore them I had to be realistic and strong.

I so wanted this relationship to last forever, but I knew I still had a long way to go. We both did, and so we ended the relationship after four months. It hurt a lot but I felt God saying 'the best is yet to be'. This person so enhanced my life, in word, music, song, love, etc. It was another 'pre-taster' of what could be and despite the pain I count it a blessing. For me, it was time to heal and rest. And so with this pre-taster in mind I continue to press into God for ALL He has for me.

I learned intimacy is not just sex. Before I'd only felt loved when I 'made love'. This relationship showed me I didn't have to make love to be loved. Intimacy was an openness of thoughts, honesty, body, mind, soul, spirit, a sharing of oneself – being allowed to be oneself – no holds barred. Not demanding or conditional. And since, I have walked a day at a time constantly learning, being made whole again. I have no desire to go into any relationship and not give my heart – fully, totally, I want to love always as if I'd never been hurt.

There were few things I could not do – at least that's what I had thought.

With the summer arriving, and the grass and hedge growing, I realised I would have to venture to the shed! The lawnmower was relatively easy to master, but I had a profound fear of hedge trimmers! (Maybe it was a result of watching too many horror movies as a child or their resemblance to chainsaws – who knows!) I knew I had to overcome this! My brother-in-law came over and provided my first lesson on how to use them. With fear and trembling I took my first swipe and I've not looked back since. Afterwards I felt such triumph – I had cut the hedge (it looked as if it had been brutally attacked BUT it was cut!). To others, it may not seem a particularly amazing feat, but my fear was gone. After that I was given a 'jigsaw' which I used to saw wood for the fire until I was too adventurous and attempted a tree – the jigsaw gave up but I continued on. Ripsaws, power tools, strimmers, I was on a roll! I worked hard in the garden, keeping it and although I'm not finished I find such pleasure in it. I'll never make a landscape gardener or a DIY specialist but I'm not afraid to try!

I learned to check the oil, water, air and 'scooshers' in my car – I even bought a Haynes manual (in the event the local garage is closed and I have to work out what to do) – I'll never make an AA engineer but I'm not afraid to try!

I learned not to panic when the boiler broke down, the electrics went off, the car wouldn't start, the plumbing leaked, the guttering broke, but I took it all one step at a time, and God has made a way for me to no longer fear.

I rarely noticed my surroundings or the pleasure they could bring. Somehow it had all become so complicated. God came and told me to keep it simple. I had become so busy for Him I never saw Him. No more! I have laid it all down and I'm keeping it simple.

Conclusion

Mostly God has revealed areas to me. Although difficult to face the truth about myself, I have continued on in this journey of discovery. There have been many times when I have cried out, 'Stop, I can't take anymore; I can't face anymore'. A 'rest period' has ensued, then I continue on.

In the meantime I'm enjoying this new-found love of life. I have nothing of great worth, materially, but I have a peace within my being which I consider priceless. I strive not for things, but am content whether I have little or a lot. It's hard at times, as I can't be as generous with gifts, and it is difficult when I see a stunning outfit or a gorgeous pair of shoes, but I enjoy life more so it's worth it!

The songs and poems have come at different times in my life but I rarely shared them. It was never my intention to do anything with them, but then when I did share them people were moved by them or encouraged by them. Through their encouragement, and now believing God hasn't given me these gifts to hide, I'm stepping up to share what I have.

It's amazing what I see — I appreciate so much now. I have everything even though I have less. I really have more than ever. I enjoy long barefoot walks on the beach, writing in the sand, walking in the rain till I'm soaked through to the skin, building a log fire to warm me and just watching the fire burn, walking in the snow and building a snow gal, watching the birds come to eat at the table, knocking down a wall, lifting a patio, laying a path, mowing the lawn, trimming the hedge, swinging an axe, using a circular saw, collecting and cutting wood, checking the oil and water in my car.

To walk the hills where there is no path with just a map and compass to guide, to enjoy sunrises and sunsets, to delight in family and friends, I jump up and down on my mattress, I cycle my bike down country roads, I've ridden on a motorbike (as a passenger), driven a quad (although I can't change gear!) most recently realised my fear of animals had diminished and helped feed deer, cattle and sheep with them all around me, without screaming blue murder, or freezing on the spot and having to be carted off like something from the wax museum. I wear coloured shoes, paint my toenails red, walk in high heels.

The creativity that used to come out only in my darkest hours is out in daylight! Such is the work that God has done in my life; I could never have got through without His love, His support, His guidance. To simplify life and live it, enjoying it rather than enduring it.

And so, here I am, with a few songs, some poems, a new appreciation of life, I take time to breathe. All of this is possible because God loves me so much, even when beaten by the Roman guards, He lifted His head and said 'I will not give up or give in – I've got to have them with me for eternity!' He didn't just die on a cross and leave it at that, He is concerned about my life, He cares that life had become too much and slowed me down.

He has taught me to love, to sing, to laugh, to dance, to create, to write, to worship, to enjoy, to believe again, He has taught me how to live. There's a new horizon – a new day is awakening so if you hear God saying 'Come and take a walk with me' don't be afraid to go - remember 'the best is yet to be...'

I don't know what the future holds but I know who holds my future!

I will dare to believe!

Will you?

Written during The Preparation

I Started on This Journey

I started on this journey
a long time ago
And where this path would lead me
I just didn't know
I'd lived my life as I wanted to
going my own way
Until I met with Jesus
in a very special way
He gave me love
like I had never know
Wrapped me in His loving arms
and called me to His own
He gave me a new life
and a reason to go on
And filled my life with meaning
And put within my heart a song

Like a Bird

I was like a bird trapped and caged
and my wings were broken
but words of life and freedom
into my life You've spoken.
You saw me in this place
so afraid and all alone
and You sent Your son Jesus.
For my sin He did atone.
You've opened up the door
and set my wings in place
so I can fly freely
in Your strength and grace.
I'll soar just like the eagle
I'll mount on eagle's wings
for peace and love into my life
is what Your presence brings

Many times in my life through various people, the symbolism of a trapped bird has been used and they knew nothing of my life or circumstances. It is only now I understand for I was so used to the 'cage' I never realised I was imprisoned within myself but now I'm free from it, I see so clearly and realise the happiness I had was fleeting and dependent upon people and circumstances but now the happiness within is there independently. Do I still have bad days? Yes! Am I always laughing? No! For I have discovered happiness is not a jovial, free of trouble state but contentment within. There is a 'rest' within my being I had never known…until now and its God alone who gives such rest!

The Lord bless you and keep
you
The Lord make His face shine
upon you
and be gracious to you
Numbers 6:24

My Prayer

Teach me Your ways
that I might walk in Your truth.
Give me a pure heart
that I might honour You
with all my heart.
I will praise You o Lord my God.
I will give glory
to You forever
for Your love for me
is so very great
you have rescued me
from the depths of darkness

The Beach

The beach is deserted
and I sit alone
wondering why
he stays at home.
'No rest is needed!'
is his reply
to my questions.
'Why?, why?, why?'
I've walked for miles
so I'm having a seat
and paddled in the surf
to cool my feet.
I'm only just over
from where I'm staying.
My inevitable return
I am just delaying.
For once I go in I won't want to come out.
I'll just stay in my room -
of that there's no doubt.
Read through the pages
of books that I've brought
or write odes like this -
quite a few I have got -
but still the question
remains in my head:
would he be happier if I were dead?
For then he could work
as he does just now
but without my complaining,
my why, my how.
And so I sit
alone on the beach
and answers to questions
remain out of reach.
Now there's the rain -
I'd better head off.
See you later,
Ta ta, and sod off!

The Spider

The spider he wandered in
around quarter past eight
not knowing what
would be his fate.
Round by the heater
and along the fireplace
he slowly meandered
but then quickened his pace.
Something up
in the distance ahead
had only slept,
it was not dead.
He faltered and waited,
frozen still
on the hump of the carpet
he thought a hill.
Again he moved
and ventured on
But the 'thing' moved again,
it was not gone
What would he do?
Only time would tell.
Until the scotch tape
from the table fell.
At that he knew
ahead was danger
and of the likes
he was no stranger
so as fast as you like,
he did a u-turn
And back along the fireplace
he did burn

It was then I wondered
why he had chose the pace
so slow and meandering
when he could so race?
I guess he wanted
to see all he could
whilst out and about
in his search for food.
Each day holds danger,
some seen, some not,
but if you rush, never looking,
what have you got?
Don't fly through this life
as though in a race.
Enjoy it a bit
and the thrill of the chase.
The spider, he only does
for now and here.
He doesn't hide away,
trembling in fear,
so, from his example,
why not take a hint?
Get out there and if trouble comes – run like the wind

This was written as I had taken time out which was rare at that time for me but I realised if I didn't then sanity would not remain with me and learned things even from a spider that ventured into my room!

forgetting what is
past and looking
forward to what
lies ahead

Philippians 3.13

Live Each Day

Live each day as if it were your last.
Live each day forgetting what is past.
Live each day pressing on toward the goal.
Live each day, live it to the whole.

Leave yesterday behind you.
No need to take it with you.
Just leave it there behind you.
Don't let it keep and bind you

Live each day for the moment it provides.
Live each day for the One who guides.
Live each day with meaning and with love.
Live each day giving thanks to God above.

I wrote this less than two weeks after my Dad's death. His death just emphasised to me how I was not living life but merely 'existing'. It was after this I decided to no longer put off until tomorrow what I could do today.

The Peacock

The peacock he stands
beautiful and proud
whilst the female,
unimpressed in a shroud.
As I approached
he spread his feathers,
and this I believe
he does in all weathers.
The peahen seemed to say
'I've seen it all before'
and turned her back
before he did more.
I thought that this
was just a bit sad.
She couldn't see the good,
only the bad.
How often in life
when surrounded by beauty
do we miss what's in front of us
because it's our duty.

Open your eyes
and take a fresh look around
and you'll be amazed
by what you have found.
The peacock -
he's only showing his best
so that you'll love him
not just be impressed.
So look at your peacock
and appreciate
his beauty, his strength
for he is really great.
For all of us in life
can make a mistake.
It's best to forgive
even for our own sake.
So lay aside your shroud
of hurt and defeat,
forgive and move on -
you'll be in for a treat.
For this life is short
so live and learn
and check our your peacock
when he next does a turn

As I watched these two beautiful birds I saw myself in the peahen and how I no longer noticed or appreciated the things of life and even though I had been hurt, I had to forgive and look again with 'fresh' eyes and just love!

When the darkness fills my senses....

Leave Me Not

Leave me not
alone this day.
Come to my help,
O Lord I pray,
For no more
can I now endure
of this, Lord,
I am so sure.
So hard and painful
has been this path
sometimes I wonder
is it love or wrath
that allows these tests
to carry on.
Please God, I pray,
let them be gone
that I could find comfort
and peace once more
and joy and delight
at what you have in store.
Please, Lord I pray give me a break -
this I ask for my own sake

Worry weighs a person down;
an encouraging word cheers a
person up

Proverbs 12:25

Sleep...less

I try for hours
but sleep won't come
I toss and turn
and my legs are numb.
My arms are sleeping
but not my head.
My mind is awake
but my body is dead.
Why can't I sleep
when I am so tired?
If sleep were a job,
I would surely be fired.
Boil the milk
and give the hot choc a whisk.
Insomnia is here,
of sleep there's no risk.
Here I lie
on the settee
Whilst sleeping soundly
next door is he.
Sometimes I read,
sometimes I don't.
I just try to rest
since my body won't.
The fish tank it bubbles
and gurgles away,
And Fred swims about
in his own sweet way.
It's quiet outside,
most people in bed
O how I wish
I was asleep instead

LOVE IS PATIENT

KIND

IS NOT JEALOUS

IS NOT BOASTFUL

NOT PROUD

NOT RUDE

NOT IRRITABLE

KEEPS NO RECORD

UNCONDITIONAL

SUFFERS LONG

BEARS ALL THINGS

BELIEVES ALL THINGS

HOPES ALL THINGS

ENDURES ALL THINGS

LOVE NEVER FAILS AND WILL LAST FOREVER

Written during Revelation and Restoration

I Wonder

What do you think when you look at us,
so busy with our lives; always making a fuss
and never giving you a second thought,
when it was with your son our freedom was bought?
This is what I often wonder…
This is what I often wonder…

What do you see when you look at life?
Did you meant it to be filled with all this strife,
or is this the result of man's desire to rebel,
or lack of fear of going to hell?
This is what I often wonder…
This is what I often wonder…

I see so much heartache, pain and fear.
People never stopping to shed a tear
for the poor and needy they leave on the street
with barely warm clothes and holed shoes on their feet.
This is what I often wonder…
This is what I often wonder…

Where is this world going with its war and hate?
What will be its end? What is its fate?
Will all be destroyed when you can take no more?
Or will you come again and your love outpour?
This is what I often wonder…
This is what I often wonder…

Restless

My mind goes wild
and my head is sore
and as each day passes
it's filled even more
with thoughts of work
and thoughts of life.
So much turmoil,
pain and strife,
if only it would all
go quiet inside
And to a place of rest
I could go and hide,
so this could all
wash over me,
and from the torment
I'd be free.
I long to rest
and easy sleep,
to no longer lie awake,
to no longer weep
but as night creeps in,
sleep moves out
and my head is full of turmoil,
full of doubt.
No matter how I try
to rest or sleep
it's just not happening
and I remain a heap
of emotions and hormones
going wild
like a small and very
over-tired child.
Maybe one day
the peace will come

And the thoughts and cares
will be struck dumb
And rest shall again
be part of my day.
And the pain
shall simply fade away.
But for now
I need to go get a pill
'cause of this headache.
I've had my fill
So I shall rest my pencil down
at least for now
And go give this head
a superhero's 'kapow'!

I HAVE CALLED YOU BY NAME AND YOU ARE MINE... YOU ARE HONOURED AND I LOVE YOU

ISAIAH 43:1-4

Who Am I

Who am I?
Who am I without you in my life?
Why have I found favour in your eye?
Who am I, without You, who am I
Before I was conceived
You knew and planned for me
In the secret place,
You formed and fashioned me
To be Your child,
for now,
to be Your child
But what have I to offer?
What could make a start?
I have nought of worth to give you
but my heart
my soul
my life
my all.
You are my all in all.

I have often wondered why the God of creation should care for me, who am I?
His answer always comes, full of love and re-assurance
'you are my child, my creation, the apple of my eye and I love you!'

OF WORTH

PREPARED

CALLED

FORMED

LOVED

MINE..

BLESSED

YOUR CHILD

70

FASHIONED

Make a Difference?

If I write it down does it change anything?
Is it any different to see it in ink?
Than to hear it in voice?
Does it make it any more or any less
than it is?
Does it make you think more of it?
As you are reminded by the written word
when the voice has long gone in the silence,
the voice can give a tone or a depth
that can cut ... or can soothe,
but when the memory holds it no longer
It's gone ... it's forgotten.
The pen it writes, and the words may fade
but can still be seen
to remind you of what once was
of what could have been.
If only you'd listened to that voice,
if only you'd read the words of the pen.
You don't hear the voice anymore;
It's faded in the shadows.
You see the words and ... regret?
Maybe, maybe not.
You can always put the words aside,
so they haunt you no more.
Would it have made any difference?

I had at times wished my Dad had written to us, his daughters, as it was difficult following his death. He hadn't been a man to show affection and although we knew he loved us there were times that followed that we sought some assurance but then I thought would it have made any difference...

71

When I'm Here...

When I'm here and surrounded
by such amazing beauty
I wonder at how this world
can be filled with so much cruelty.
But then I remember
that God gave man the choice
to stand and watch in silence
or take action and raise his voice.
With every day that passes,
opportunities arise
to see what's going on
or else divert our eyes;
to be concerned with what we see
and act accordingly
or simply walk on by
because 'it's nothing to do with me'.
How often do we stop?
Have we ever taken time?
to get to know the reason why
the beggar holds that sign
'hungry & homeless -
'Please give me your spare change'?
Or do we walk on past
labelling them as deranged?
They too were born as we,
a babe so small and calm,
and life has made a path
that didn't shelter them from harm.
Maybe they made choices
that were not so very wise
but who are we to judge,
but for God's grace go I.
So I lay aside my thoughts
and cares about this life
and just walk in the midst of majesty,
forgetting this world's strife.
If only for the moment,
in this place I find such rest
And thank my God above,
for I am truly blessed

At the time of writing this I was yet to discover my husband's unfaithfulness. I had so much going on in my head as it disturbed me so to see and hear people passed judgement on others less fortunate and labelling them without knowing 'the story'.

73

For Such a Time as This!

For such a time as this, my friend,
He has called You to His side.
He has planned for this moment,
and prepared you as His bride.
For such a time as this, my friend,
He's planned this path for you,
that you would seek His heart
in everything you do.
For such a time as this my friend,
for such a time as this.
How can you fight it?
How can you resist?
For such a time as this my friend
For such a time as this.

The story of Esther in the bible spoke to me as she was not of noble birth or of great 'worth' yet she found herself in a place of influence quite unexpectedly and could choose to remain silent or take a stand. She chose to stand even if it meant her death and her uncle spoke to her and said 'who knows but it could be you were put in place for such a time as this'. None of us truly know the influence we have in the lives of those around us. We may not find ourselves in a palace but rest assured the decisions we make and the lives we live have far reaching effects!

I Have Learned

Since you left there's much I have learned,
much I have learned about me,
why I was the way I was,
always hoping you'd love me.

Sometimes I see it was an impossible task
for to love me you'd have to love yourself
so in your search for 'happiness true'
you found another and put me on the shelf.

I find it hard to understand or comprehend
how you lived a lie for so long.
I suppose you struggled and tried to stay;
you've left me now and you are gone.

I need to let you go and this is so hard,
for to you I promised to be true.
I gave you my love, my heart and my all.
I really did love you.

YOU WILL NO LONGER LIVE IN SHAME...
...THE SHAME OF YOUR WIDOWHOOD WILL BE
REMEMBERED NO MORE...
...FOR YOUR CREATOR WILL BE YOUR
HUSBAND...
...AS A YOUNG WIFE ABANDONED BY HER
HUSBAND...
...WITH EVERLASTING LOVE I WILL HAVE
COMPASSION ON YOU...
...NEVER AGAIN!...
...I WILL REMAIN LOYAL TO YOU...
...I WILL REBUILD YOU...
...YOUR ENEMIES WILL STAY AWAY...
...YOU WILL LIVE IN PEACE...
...I AM ON YOUR SIDE...
...MY COVENANT OF BLESSING WILL NEVER BE
BROKEN...

ISAIAH 54

The Message

The message it spoke of 'divorce' and 'affair';
in that moment was realised my worst nightmare.
Shocked to my core and shaking to the bone,
as for the first time in my life I checked his phone.
What do I do? What do I say?
Do I hide that I know? Will it make it go away?
A mixture of emotions surge through my being;
it's too surreal to believe what I'm seeing.
There's no point hiding it, so I showed him his phone,
and asked him to confirm I'd been right all along.
He'd lied, he'd cheated and made me believe I was mad.
The fact I'd been right just made me so sad.
His reaction was shock for he'd been found out,
and all his self-assurance soon turned to doubt.
Panic set in and he avoided the truth;
so many lies just poured from his mouth

Self justification and 'unimportant was she';
'just don't do anything till I get home' said he,
but as it dawned on me right then and there,
our marriage was in trouble and going nowhere.
So many incidents fell into place
as I stood and looked at his ashen face.
I'd always loved him and now was the same -
'tell me it all and tell me her name.'
I suggested he move out and take his time
to decide what he wanted, by her side or mine,
but take the time alone, don't see her or me.
He left our home and to work he did flee.
I stood in disbelief at what had begun:
 the betrayal, the rejection, the pain, his shun.
I dialled the number as I fell to my knees,
'he's been having an affair – help me please!'

God showed me to pray and also to fast;
for the next ten days that did last.
Rarely sleeping, new hope did arise
for God had revealed truth and uncovered the lies.
On that first night he returned to our home,
and took all his clothes and promised to phone.
Seeing him leave so broke me inside
I cried out to God, 'please, let me hide!'
At that moment as I stood alone
I started to worship but I couldn't condone
the actions he'd taken were so very wrong,
but God had prepared for it and gave me a song.
As my husband walked out and I lay on the floor
sobbing and broken, God walked in the door.
He lifted me gently, 'my child, come and rest
and believe me when I say, I know what is best.'

I felt relief that I'd finally found out,
for the lies revealed left no shadow of doubt.
I wasn't insane, I wasn't losing my mind,
my instinct had been right and I hadn't been blind.
I determined in my heart to pray faithfully
until it was known what the decision would be,
but days rolled past and no call was made
and I realised then it was a game he played.
Not wanting to decide he claimed he didn't know,
'there's too much going on, I'm busy' was his woe.
So I asked if he'd seen her and his answer was 'yes',
'well it's over for us, is what you're saying more or less.'
What he did next I couldn't believe;
he took her out in public for all to see.
It had been five days since he had left,
and this action of his left me completely bereft

Making his statement, 'I'll do what I want
and no one will stop me' became his taunt.
'I have a right to be happy and to hell with the rest,'
and he trampled me down like some grubby pest.
We managed a meeting to discuss what to do;
he still couldn't tell me our marriage was through.
Our meeting was surreal but the best talk we had,
 for after that day his attitude was bad.
He treated me dreadfully and so unfair;
I found it hard to believe that he just didn't care.
Maybe it was a defence, maybe just him,
for he'd been wearing a mask that had worn thin;
when we last went away, time spent north,
I saw he was running for all he was worth.
He told me it was nothing, but I saw that he'd changed,
once such a loving guy, now almost deranged.

It had been on our return from New Year break
that he told me 'no children, not ever, no way.'
I was crushed for yet again he'd led me to believe
and all he could say was 'are you going to leave?'
The next 24 hours were torture for me,
letting go what we'd planned, to stay or to flee.
I got on my knees and asked God what to do.
He told me to stay and said 'I'll protect you'
I went out that day encouraged by God's word,
For I believed my cry He had heard.
I had laid my dreams that day in God's hand,
and gave away the maternity clothes for that had been 'canned.'
I set in my heart to fervently pray
for my husband early each day,
for God to protect but reveal what was hid
and on any secrets, to lift the lid.

In just ten days the affair was revealed
although the details he still concealed.
He avoided contact and refused to talk;
to discuss it was impossible, for it made him baulk.
He didn't even tell me that we'd come to an end;
I had to hear it from family and friend.
A couple of months later he managed to text me,
saying it was over and that he'd left me.
I determined from the beginning that I would get through;
how I would do it, I just never knew.
But my faith and hope were in God above,
for I knew that His heart toward me was love.
I didn't and still don't want to be bitter,
and whilst away hours and carelessly fritter
time that I could spend growing in this
to come out healed and whole – what bliss!

I've learned so much since he walked out my life,
had to face facts and have gone through such strife,
but determined am I not to fall apart
but to regain and renew so I can still give my heart.
I have no regrets and this is the truth,
there are days that are bad and days that are good,
for facing this pain and working it through,
really takes so much out of you.
'Don't cry because it's at an end
– but smile because to you it happened.'
And I'm glad we had love for so many years
even though it ended with so many tears.
I had the choice to forgive or to hate;
I chose the first from the very first date
for I'd made a vow to love come what may,
to walk this life as best, God's way

He moved away, returned to his parent's abode
and on the day he left I imagined the road.
He'd never travelled it without me by his side,
and I wondered if he thought of me on that ride,
but then the pain hit, as I knew he wasn't alone;
he was taking this girl to his family home.
How his parents could allow it I just didn't know -
the hurt that I felt I had to let go.
It was then I realised and gave up my hope
that we'd be reconciled – was there chance? Nope!
The decision to divorce was the hardest I'd made
for I had promised to love always and now I was afraid.
I'd never imagined that we would part
for it had been for always I'd given my heart,
and here I was faced with life without him
and my future seemed suddenly dim.

But God stepped in and brought His light,
'don't be afraid, this is not your fight,
For I will win this battle on your behalf,
there will be days again when you will laugh,
but for now, I need you to rest and to wait,
while I work in your life for it's not your fate;
It is Me who works to will and to do,
and if you trust in Me I'll get you through.'
So that's what I've done and will continue to do;
it's not been easy but I will get through
for it is God who turns bad for good,
curse into blessing and from famine brings food.
For God I am thankful, He's so blessed my life,
He's given me family and friends to help in the strife
I have peace for the past and hope for tomorrow
for only He can bring joy out of such sorrow

So if you find yourself in events of the same,
don't let the circumstances take you out of the game
but cry out to God in your grief and despair.
He'll be your strength for He says ' I care! '
When bad things happen we seek to blame,
someone, anyone, no one, God's name.
Yet we grow so much in the toughest of time,
we just don't see it till we've made the climb,
and from the heights we see the path,
and understand it was of love – not wrath -
that God led us and kept us safe,
that we might be strengthened and build our faith.
So this day settle in your heart
to follow God and not depart
for the path He has chosen is specific to you -
He's holding your hand and He'll get you through.

The Lord is close to the broken-hearted

This is Not How I Imagined...

This is not how I imagined it would be.
This is not what I had dreamed of or hoped for.
When I found you I was so grateful.
When I found you I knew I wanted to live this life out.
When I found you I chose to love you.
No matter what...no matter when...no matter how
I would love you always.
I wanted to grow old loving you.
I wanted to grow old with you loving me.
And now I'm in a place I never imagined I'd be.
I had never thought there would be a time we'd not be together.
I never contemplated we'd ever part.
I never thought you'd leave and walk away.
I never considered this life without you.
I never thought you'd give up on us.
But you did.
And here I am...broken.
Here I am...crushed.
Here I am...devastated.
Here I am...confused.
Here I am...searching for answers.
Answers you will not give.
Reasons you will not say.
Causes I cannot see.
All you say is it's not me.
True you changed your mind.
True you chose to give up on us.
True you chose to walk away.
True you chose to betray our love.
True you chose to betray our trust.
True you chose to break your promises.
True you chose to break your vows.
True you chose to find another.
Is that the only kind of 'love' you understand?
One who 'needed' you?
You could not accept love pure and raw.
Love for who you were,
love not for what you did,
love not for need but just love,
a love that would not let you go

no matter what you did,
no matter what you said,
no matter what happened,
a love that remained constant.
You had this gift of love in me and you threw it aside.
This gift of love in me you trampled underfoot
with no thought, no regard.
This I see but fail to understand how
how you could not see,
how you could not tell.
I believe one day you will see,
you will see what you had,
what you had and what you threw away.
On that day you will gasp,
you will gasp at what was yours,
what was yours and what you threw aside,
what you threw aside and left behind.
On that day I pray God gives you peace,
peace in facing what you had,
peace in facing what you lost.
May peace be yours on that day
but for now
I must somehow find a way to let you go,
I must somehow find the strength to say goodbye,
I must somehow find a way to move on from this place,
this place of brokenness,
this place of shattered hopes,
this place of darkness and despair.
I know there will be a day
I will awaken and all will be well within.
The ashes of my life will have within it glowing embers
that will be rekindled and reignite
to a blazing flame once again,
that love would once again be restored,
not between you and I
for that love will remain but not the same
…never the same
but a love within me that loves as if it's never been hurt
for I have learned that truly…
it is better to have loved and lost
than to have never loved at all

Here I Sit

Here I sit,
looking out at the glistening sea
like diamonds sparkling
such beauty.
A bird calls out.
Who knows the message it says?
The sun is warm and
there's a gentle breeze blowing
there's a rustling with each gust,
a wrapper of sorts caught
the tide gently lapping the sand.
On days like this
it's easy to forget the heartache and yet...
at the same time remind me of the heartache
for days like this are for sharing
but you are gone and we share no more...

Alone with My Thoughts

Alone with my thoughts
but not alone
for You are with me
all along.
My Father, my Friend,
My Beloved,
You have ravished my heart,
O Lord.
I am Yours,
And You are mine.
I am glad
I love You.
I'm learning to know You more
and the more I know You
the more I love You.
I am Yours
and You are mine

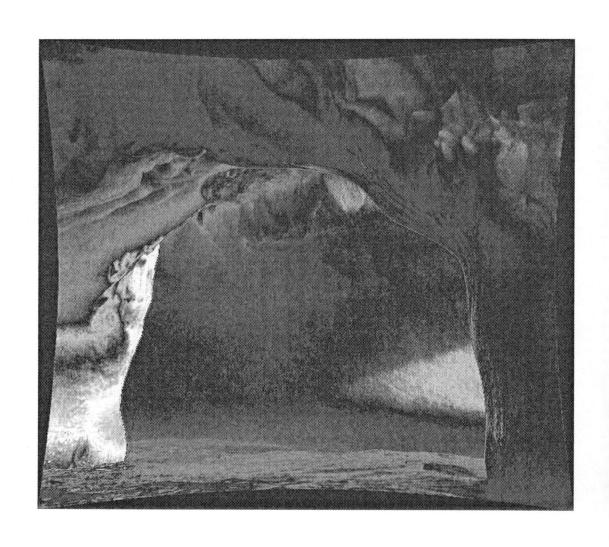

Is There a Place I Can Go and Scream?

Is there a place that I can go and scream?
For this cannot be happening,
this must be a dream.
He's gone, he's left,
he's walked right out my life,
telling me he loved me,
but just not as his wife.
How do I handle this?
How do I move on?
The pain that overwhelms me
ever since he's gone -
my life was him
and all I hoped to be.
My dreams lay shattered on the floor
the day that he left me
but on that day of his departure
as I lay on the floor
completely overwhelmed and broken,
God walked in the door.
He took me oh so gently,
into His arms of care
and held me tight into Him
as I lay sobbing there.
What have I got?
And who on earth am I?
My husband has deserted me
and said no reason why.
"YOU ARE MINE MY CHILD, TO ME YOU HAVE MUCH WORTH
FOR I HAVE LOVED YOU ALWAYS, WAY BEFORE YOUR BIRTH"

Long Has Been This Path

Long has been this path and hard has been this road,
this journey of discovery that many feet have trod,
discovering You in the midst of this trial,
discovering me and the fight for survival.
I wouldn't wish this pain upon any other,
and yet I feel Your protection and I sense Your cover.
My Father and my Guide, to You I ask this day
please take me by the hand and lead me on Your way
for my heart within is breaking and I can't face alone
this path of pain and grief that causes me to groan.
Please come and be my strength, my very strong tower
and where my strength is gone, fill me with Your power
that there will come a day of freedom and of rest
when I will stand strong and I will be dressed
with the garments of salvation and sing a song of praise,
for though I fell and wept, I once again was raised,
for the enemy didn't realise that when he crushed me down
You would lift me up and place upon my head a crown.
His plan for me was harm but Yours for me was good
and when this battle is over he'll wish he'd understood
a life within God's hand is a force with which to be reckoned.
Do not walk away when you hear Him to you beckon
for God will be your rampart, your fortress and your guide.
He will lead you safely and never leave your side
His heart is always for you, He made you, you're His child
His love is ever toward you, it cannot be reviled
and so this day be strong and do not stop the race
for when you finish here, in heaven you have a place

Help Me to Rise

Help me to rise above
the memories and pain
that I might find love
and passion once again.
Father, I am broken -
this hurt is just too sore;
please heal me and hold me
for I can take no more.
Please bring me comfort
a peace and a calm
that I might lay it all
within your palm,
for my life is Yours.
I'm Your daughter and child;
grant me peace
in the storm and the wild
that out of the ashes
I will arise and come forth
to finally know in You
what I am worth

When I'm Surrounded

When I'm surrounded by such amazement
I find it so hard to believe
that almost four months ago
you chose to go and leave.
The days crawl by so slowly
but then there's some go fast
It seems so surreal;
you're becoming part of my past.
For the time we had together
I thank my God above
for when I was with you
I learned how to love,
not the shallow floaty kind
but the deep unconditional sort
that held in hell and high water,
even when you hit 'abort'.
I don't really know the reasons;
I try to hazard a guess
but I'll never know what happened
to make you love me less.
It's hard to let you go
when my life was so one with yours
since my heart still feels so strongly;
for broken hearts there are no cures
but I must release you from me
and disentangle myself from you
for we are no longer one;
from here on in we're two.
The wrenching that has happened
has left me feeling torn,
My emotions are a roller coaster
and my face is looking worn.
There are things that I have learned,
about myself and you,
That I wouldn't have believed
or even said were true,
But since you left that day
it's made me stop and look
And 'growing through divorce'
has been such an insightful book.

We both had such deep needs
we couldn't even see
but in all our marriage,
I really loved you…
You have made the choice
to no longer share this life
Or keep your promise to me;
you don't want me as your wife
for you have gone back home
to stay with your mum and dad,
and of course, your girlfriend.
That makes me really sad
for I thought we had a love
that was strong and that would last
but even that has become
a thing that's in the past.
A day has happened
I never thought I'd see -
We have parted ways
and you've forgotten me.
And so with this I'll end
wishing you happiness and love
and for the time we had
I thank my God above

His Passion & Crime

Such was his passion
this was His crime
that He loved us so dearly
He paid for your sin and mine.
It's His heart that is for us
that we should come to know
Our Father in heaven
Who loves us so.

The Lone Footballer

The lone footballer practices late.
The dusk it settles down;
it's twilight and I watch
as he kicks the ball around.
I stand and wonder
'does he wish someone there with him?
To help his practice, to kick and tackle,
as the night draws in'
I stand alone watching his antics,
wishing I were there
just to have the company,
but go I do not dare,
and so I watch from afar
as he does his stuff
wondering when he'll call it a night
and say enough's enough.
I leave the window
and watch his play no more
as I carry on about my business
going from floor to floor
I open the window upstairs
and hear the ball being played
and somehow I am comforted
even though no word is said.
knowing someone's there
makes all the difference to me,
even though we're strangers
and never again may see,
but for tonight, from him,
some kind of peace
I get from his being there,
I simply feel release.

There were times of such overwhelming and intense loneliness; this was written on one of those nights...

Freedom

Bound by all I thought I should be,
the things of life they fashioned me,
the people around me, and the opinion of man,
kept me in chains and out of Your plan.
There came a day You drew me aside
and showed me in You I could confide
my deepest pains, my darkest sorrow,
the guilt of yesterday and fears for tomorrow.
Freedom is the place You're taking me to -
free to be me, created by You
free to laugh
free to sing
free to dance;
my praise I'll bring
for You are making me free

As I came to discover, I had lived my life in fear, in living up to other's expectations and if I wasn't 'doing' or 'caring' for others I was worthless.

God stopped this merry-go-round and took me off so that I could find my worth in Him.

In the early days I came across one of Susan Lordi's willow tree figures called 'Happiness' and it stated under 'free to sing..to laugh, to dance...create'. I bought it and prayed that one day I would stand as this figure able to sing as if no-one were listening, to dance as if no one were watching and to laugh heartily...

I thank God, I can now stand as this figure singing, dancing, laughing and creating!

Sitting on The Beach...

Sitting on the beach tonight and listening to the song,
knowing I'm Your child and I didn't do it wrong,
I lived my life before You and would have carried on,
but he didn't want to be a part of that and now he has gone.
I wish it could be different and I didn't have this pain
but realise You're with me and with You there will be gain.
Please Lord help me through this, help me to let go
that I can move beyond this place because You love me so.
I do not want to live my life with any regret
so help me deal with this and to no longer fret
for I am only responsible for this life of mine
and for the choices that I make in this given time.
I cannot change the actions or the things that others do -
only they can answer when their lives are before You,
so I hand this boulder over, of false responsibility
and bring it all before You, that You might set me free.
Hear the cry within me, my heart it longs for You,
that I might soar above this life and all will become new
for You have truly loved me and ravished my heart.
I know that You have called me and that I'm set apart,
for such a time as this You've said, You called me to Your side
that I may walk with You and You will be my Guide,
my Protector and my Comfort, my Father and my Friend.
You will see me safely to this journey's end,
so I will not be discouraged but I will stand in faith
and fly the victory flag, and the banner I will raise
for as long as I am able I will walk with You
for You are my Beloved, Faithful One and true
and from this life I've learned, lessons I can share
to help others on this journey and show people that You care
about all the facets of their lives, nothing is too small
for You love the same, everyone and all.

I Know I'm Getting Better...

I know I'm getting better,
I know I'm growing strong
but there are days that go slowly
and time goes on so long.
The emotions come and take me,
on a journey I've come to know
but deep within my heart
I know You love me so
for You Lord are my comfort,
my rock, my strength, my friend.
You will never leave me,
on You I can depend
and this I've learned so deeply
and come to know of late
for You have been my husband,
and kept my love from hate.
You've changed my life so much
that I can honestly say
even though I don't understand,
I know You'll make a way
In what may seem impossible,
and when all around say's 'no'
because of what You've promised,
You will make it so.
And so I want to say thank you
for giving my life new hope
and filling my heart with strength
when I felt I couldn't cope,
for in the days gone past
I would've taken the easy way out
but You've filled my life with meaning
and removed from me my doubt
for before I couldn't believe
that I was worth the love
but You've opened the windows of heaven
and showered me from above.
You've replaced my fear with trust
and my insecurity with peace.
You've given me a reason
and caused my striving to cease
for my life, it is a gift,

that You have given me.
I now give back to You
that I might be free
for it's in the letting go,
that gifts take on their role
not holding them tightly to you,
for that strain takes its toll.
Allow your gift the freedom,
the space in which to grow
and watch how much more fruitful
and how your gift does grow

The last section of this poem was written with the story of Hannah in mind. Her heart's desire was for a child and she cried out for many years and eventually she had a son. Rather than clinging to what she had always sought and desired, she dedicated him to God and from a very young age he served in the temple. Samuel became one of the greatest prophets known in history – would it have been the same had she kept him at home?

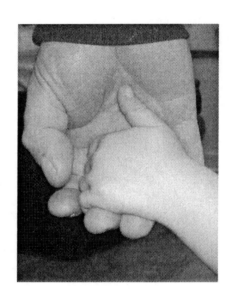

Lord I'm Glad You're in My Life

Lord I'm glad You're in my life;
You are my hope, my strength in the strife;
You erase my fears and my doubts You clear;
I can face anything with You near.
Bad days come and I take a blow
but You've given me friends who are in the know
and I don't know how but they help me lift
for these friends from You are truly a gift.
There are times of late I've wanted to run
to hide, to scream, but to You I turn.
There's nothing more I want or desire
than to be with You, to move up higher.
This desire's so strong it turns me inside out
to be used by You and to never doubt
the love You have for me, the future in You
is for my good, it really is true.
I try to imagine how it'll be,
how will it work? How will I be free?
But I have to rest and trust You to do
the work You have to, to get me through
so I'm gonna try and be patient and wait for You
to complete this renovation in me to be through.
Sometimes I can't wait to see what You've planned
but I'll wait, and walk, and take Your hand;
my heart is for You, for Your will for me
for I know it's only in You I can be truly free.
The taste I had was so profound
I'm hungry for You, my cry resounds;
if heaven were here I'd pound on the door
and run to where You are for of You I want more.
You're my reason for living, my heartbeat, my breath.
There's nothing can keep me from You, not even death.
My Father, my King, my Husband, My Friend
You're my everything, the One on whom I can depend.
My life without You is not worth the thought,
my heart is Yours, with Your blood it is bought,
and so Lord I'm glad You're in my life,
for You are my hope, my strength in the strife.

My Father, Dear Father

My Father, dear Father, please help me this day -
people speaking of him really blows me away.
It's so hard to think that to him I was nothing;
he's moving on so fast, it really does sting.

To imagine him there with his parents and girl
really makes my heart ache and my head whirl;
It makes me think I had no value or worth.
Death has arrived where I thought would be birth.

Help me move on, help me let go,
so to think of him at all won't hurt me so.
I just don't understand how he could do what he's done -
We are now two instead of one.

Show me some hope of what my life holds;
please give me reason, let my future unfold
that I can keep going, one step at a time.
Help me remember I'm Yours and You're mine.

Father, my Father, please hold my heart;
for today it feels like it's coming apart,
tossed back and forth like the waves of the sea,
my thoughts are so transient, please let me be.

Father, dear Father, please help me this day,
I give You my pain that you will take it away,
that I might move on and grow strong in You
I know that You're able to get me through.

'I have prayed for you that your faith will not fail' [Luke 22:32]

Build Me a Place in Your Heart

Build me a place in your heart
where I can come and dwell.
Follow the plans that I give
that it might be well,
for I will give you all you need,
this covenant we share;
build me a place in your heart
and I will meet with you there,
for this is the time of the harvest.
Now is the time to prepare;
open your heart for my dwelling
and I will meet with you there

Based around Exodus 25:22

On Days Like Today

On days like today I wonder if you see
the overwhelming sorrow that's taking over me.
My life was like yours, not perfect but good
but all that changed before I understood
what had happened and how could it be
the husband that I loved had cheated on me?
The whirlwind of emotions tore me limb from limb
and the agony I felt did not quickly dim.
You see, I knew his faults and suspected some of the bad,
but despite it all, I truly loved the lad.
It didn't really matter, at least that's what I had thought;
he wasn't being honest, even when he was caught.
The journey that commenced was more about me
and the discoveries I've made caused me to see.
Oh I did love him, of that there was no doubt
and I loved him still, even when I found out
but me...I hated, with a passion and contempt.
Of this dislike all others were exempt
And now I have discovered in me there's good and bad.
I still try too hard at times and that knocks me flat.
I want to be whole, to be healed and to be free.
I just wish it would hurry up so I can be 'me'.
And on days like today I realise I'm not done,
It still hurts to think, I'm alone, I am one,
for I loved being a part of something intimate and unique.
I long again for a touch, to be close, cheek to cheek
to be held in arms that will love and hold dear
my heart in their hand as we two are near,
and so I'll hold fast to God and keep alive this hope
that I will find my purpose and no longer be a dope
but will walk with vision and honour giving glory to God above
and that I'll give my heart and find the gift of love.

My Father, My King

My Father, my King,
My Friend, my Everything,
There is none with which you can compare;
love like Yours is so rare.
I love and long
for the day that I'll see
Your face full of love
as I bow my knee
and listen to Your voice
as to me You declare
'well done my daughter,
your place is here
in My presence
and close by Me
where you will worship
for eternity.
My child, you are mine
you are precious to me
and I'm glad you gave
your heart willingly
for such has been your life
before My throne
I saw before time,
before you were known,
and such were the plans
that I had for your life,
it wasn't just to be a friend,
a daughter, a wife,
but the plans I made
were for you to declare
freedom to those
trapped in the snare
of the enemy's lies,
his deception and fraud,
and show them the love
of Your King and God,
and through your life
My love has been shown,
The captives set free,
And the birds have flown.

The breach is repaired,
and the binding is broken
just because you believed
in the word that was spoken,
and so now I bless you
and grant your desire
to be with me always
and move up higher
to sing in My presence
and dance before Me
to laugh and create
for NOW you are free.

Peace

I Am Overwhelmed by The Peace I Feel

I am overwhelmed by the peace I feel.
My life is not frantic, the rest is real.
Not knowing what tomorrow holds in store
no longer causes fear, I don't need to know anymore

For I rest in knowing God has a plan
and that whatever happens, He holds my hand.
The fears and doubts that once controlled my life
only caused me anxiety, stress and strife

I now take pleasure from the smallest of things,
resting in the fact that whatever life brings,
God will work it all out for my best
and so my heart can be at rest

So today I acknowledge and thank God above
for showing me mercy and His unfailing love
for without His part in my life being played
I would have remained broken, sad and afraid.

But I've been released from the bonds that held fast;
I've broken free, I've escaped at last.
My life a testimony to His support and love,
I am so grateful to my Father above

Rise up my beloved, my fair one, and come away, for the winter is past, and the rain is over and gone.

The flowers are springing up and the time of singing birds has come...

arise my beloved and come away

Song of Solomon 2:10

Who Am I That You Are Mindful of Me?

Who am I that You are mindful of me?
What do I have, what do You see?
I have nothing of great value
or of great worth
yet You have loved me
since before my birth.
You've guarded my steps
and watched over me
and worked good from bad
so beautifully.
Your hand in my life
can be so clearly seen;
without Your protection
who knows what I'd have been?
And so this day
I give You my thanks.
Were I to give money
there's not enough banks
to return back to You
what You've done for me.
Like a bird in a cage
but now been set free
I give You my appreciation
for all You have done.
My God, my Father
You are number one;
never have I known
such a faithful friend.
I'm glad You'll be with me
right to the end.
You're amazing, You're brilliant
You're faithful and true
I just want to say
My God, I love You.

The Trees

The trees they sway
as the wind blows;
They don't harden up
or refuse to move,
for if they did,
they would surely break,
but they bend
for their own sake.
How often in life
when winds come to blow
do we harden ourselves
when we should let go?
Learn to bend
and flow with the wind
for your life may one day
On it depend.

He bids you come ...

It is His Hand

It is His hand that fashions me;
it is His love that sets me free;
it is His hope that lifts my heart;
it is His faith that won't depart,
for His hand is strong to hold me fast,
for His love never ends and will always last.
His hope in me causes me to soar,
His faith opens before me even the closed door.
Of whom do I speak, I hear you say,
who is this that you speak of in this way?
It is my God, my Saviour, my King
He is my all, my everything -
His hand has lifted and carried me,
His love fills my life for all to see,
His hope has lifted me and my heart sings,
His faith has given me eagle's wings,
and so now I put my hand in His.
I bow before my Father and feel His kiss;
my hope in Him renews my sight
and by faith all darkness will become light

The Bottom Fell Out of My World

The bottom fell out of my world the other day.
I was oblivious to the trouble that had come my way.
All had appeared 'normal'; no-one could have guessed.
What happened next became one long endurance test
for life had its up, and it had its down
and we'd made it through as we stuck together, I found
but now it was you, my lover, my friend
the one on whom I thought I could depend.
We'd once shared everything in body, spirit and mind
but now you've cheated, with another, I find.
All I thought I knew was gone in a flash
and in my heart lay a deep razored gash.
As I lay bleeding from the blow
from one I'd loved but now didn't know
life could have ended for me right then and there,
but God had other plans if to believe I would dare.
As much as I thought my life was at an end,
God showed me that on Him I could depend.
'Let's get life simplified and take time to rest,
walk in obedience, and believe I know best.'
Thus started a journey of discovery for me,
of excavation and healing, restored to be free,
that I might learn through this time of despair
how to help others and show that God does care
but I couldn't do that until I found out
that He cared and loved me, to believe it without doubt.

Thank You for Your Strength

Thankyou for Your strength,
thankyou for Your care,
thankyou for believing,
and always being there.
Thankyou for Your faithfulness,
thankyou for Your truth,
thankyou for Your love,
that never can be moved.

For in the time of deepest sorrow
you never left my side.
And in the times of trouble
You gave me place to hide.
And even in the darkness,
when I could face no more,
You came into my life
and opened up the door.

Thankyou for Your mercy,
thankyou for Your grace,
thankyou for Your wisdom,
that gave me strength to face.
Thankyou for believing,
thankyou for Your love,
thankyou for Your faith,
that you showered from above.

And now I see that alls not easy,
like gold refined by fire
You're bringing forth Your champions
for Your ways are higher.
When we can find no purpose
in the trouble that we see
I hear Your voice calling
My child, just believe.

Letter to Father - I Do Not Understand

My Father, I look into Your eyes.
I stand before You and cry.
I do not understand
or know the reason why
things happen as they do
as life goes flying by,
but Lord, My King,
this much I know:
You are my reason for living
and I love You so
in all that brings
whether friendly or foe
I can be assured of safety
because You love me so.

Letter to Father - Intimacy

My Father, I look into Your eyes.
You look into mine
as You lift my face upward
and wipe away my tears.
In this moment I know
intimacy comes in these times
of broken dreams,
of shattered hopes.
You are there.
Help me to believe
to have faith
to stay open
to love;
teach me to pray
teach me Your ways

The Glimpse - Part 1

The day started early: from the church we set off,
the sun shining brightly between showers so soft.
In the car were three passengers along with me
singing as we drove through the highland scenery.

Upon approaching Glencoe an amazing sight was seen -
a rainbow, so amazing and different, so beautiful; so keen
was I to photograph this natural wonder
that covered the hillsides, it could not be a blunder.

God's word came to mind, Laura, look through the rain
beyond the clouds of doubt, of fear and pain
for the rainbow of promise was clearly displayed
and His promise of love and life was made.

I can't explain why I feel the way I do;
my heart is so drawn to the heart within you.
I don't even know you, or what kind of man
and I wonder, my Father, is this in Your plan.

For I don't want to cause pain by rushing ahead
giving life to something that should remain dead,
yet I can't explain how to you I'm compelled -
I want to get to know you and in your arms be held.

For I know I can love and I'm feeling so wary,
as this is so different and just a bit scary;
It's your heart toward God that attracts me to you:
it's thrown me in a quandary; I don't know what to do.

It goes against those unrealistic dreams.
Why is my heart like this? What does it mean?
I feel like a teenager, with a crush on a guy,
yet 'normal' conventions this does defy.

I wasn't expecting to ever feel this way,
certainly not yet, and not in this way,
but for now I'm going to leave it at the feet of God
so for my back I don't make a rod.

My Father, please show me and direct my way,
show me when to be silent and tell me what to say,
so that I do not cause pain or hurt to this man,
And bring about your purposes as only You can.

The Glimpse - Part 2

Today I feel different than I did yesterday.
I read the words that I wrote and what they convey.
I awakened wanting to know God's plan.
Is my life to be joined to this man?

I asked for a sign; to the church let him come,
knowing he'd be elsewhere so I wasn't dumb,
but then I find out he'd already been before me,
Just wasn't how I'd expected. Father, may I see?

Open my eyes to the path before me.
Don't let me falter but remain to be free.
I ask for more signs that this is Your will,
until I know from You it's hard to be still.

These things that I hear cause me to doubt.
Don't let me be stupid, just give me a clout
when it looks like I'm off down the wrong track.
Teach me to move forward and not to look back.

Help me Father, show me the way,
be my helper, my Guide, my Tower today;
keep me safely under Your wing,
and let this bird out the cage that she might sing.

The Glimpse - Part 3

Father, guide me, and lead me, I pray,
for I really don't know, so before You I lay
my fears, my anxieties, my doubts and my thoughts;
I don't want to fret because my peace it rots.

Help me to hand over the things that sidetrack,
and help me to leave it and not take it back,
but walk away and leave it in Your hands,
and grant me peace that it's all in Your plans.

It's strange cause when I'm with him nothing else matters,
but when at a distance it seems to be in tatters,
I consider how others will see it and think,
and yet it doesn't matter for between us is a link.

Father, I pray that You'd step into this place,
and set things straight and cause them to face
to sit down together and plan what to do
that they'd know Your love and plan through and through.

'Cause, Father, I do not wish to cause any pain,
nor do I want to be hurt once again.
Father, I pray, do a work for this pair,
and cause them to know how to be fair.

For me I ask Your protection and leading;
I really don't want to be wounded or bleeding.
May I continue to heal and move on from this place
and when difficulties come let me not run but face.

I give it to you, Lord, my life in Your hands
and thank you for the good that's in Your plans.
May I rest in knowing Your way;
Father, guide me and lead me, I pray.

Keep It Simple

Life had been passing me by and the enjoyment had gone.
I rarely noticed my surroundings
or the pleasure they could bring.
Somehow it had all become so complicated.
God came and told me to keep it simple.
I had become so busy for Him, I never saw Him.
No more!
Laid it all down.
Keep life simple;
It's amazing what you see.
I appreciate so much now.
I have everything even with less.
I have more than ever.
I have a car God miraculously gave me.
I have a beautiful house
that God gave me the gifts to make a home.
I have a garden in which I find so much pleasure
even when I'm just looking at it.
I enjoy long walks on the beach,
writing in the sand,
walking in the rain till I'm soaked through to the skin,
building a log fire to warm me,
and just watching the fire burn.
Walking in the snow and building a 'snowgal',
I've yet to make an angel – but that will come.
Watching the birds come to eat at the table,
knocking down a wall,
lifting a patio,
laying a path,
learning to cut a hedge,
strim a lawn.
To chop wood,
to walk the hills where there is no path,
just a map and compass to guide,
to enjoy sunrises and sunsets,
to delight in family and friends,
and all of this is possible
because my God loved me so much
He didn't just die on a cross and leave it at that
He is concerned about my life.
He cared that life had become too much,

and He slowed me down.
He has taught me to love,
to sing, to laugh, to dance,
to create, to write
to worship, to enjoy, to believe again.
He has taught me how to live.
It's a new day!
There's so much more,
were I to write it all,
I'd be old and grey,
and there would still be more
a new horizon, a new day.
The best is yet to be!

Pass Judgement

Who am I to judge and condemn
the hearts of women, the actions of men?
Have I lived so perfectly
that I have a right to pass judgement on thee?
Even Jesus didn't condemn
when the prostitute was about to be stoned by men
- 'let he who is innocent cast the first stone' -
but her actions He didn't condone,
but spoke to her and said 'go, sin no more'
and forgiveness to her He did outpour
So what right have I to hold in my heart
unforgiveness, whether in whole or in part
for I too have fallen, and received mercy and grace
so I try not to give unforgiveness a place
for it grows within and disturbs my soul
so I let it go that I might be whole!

Under Cypriot Sky

Sitting here under the Cypriot sky,
I'm amazed at how time does fly,
how life moves on and things change
and things once impossible are now within range.

You see, not so long ago I thought life was over,
I discovered my husband had taken a lover.
He was my life, my friend, my all;
it felt like I'd crashed head into a wall.

But thankfully for me, God is in control.
He will restore what the enemy stole
for His word is true and on Him you can depend
for He's not only God, He's also my friend.

He's lifted my head, and wiped away tears,
given me rest and removed all my fears,
He's given me hope and faith for each day,
and I am so glad to walk His way

And so I sit here enjoying the warmth of the sun,
And no longer think my life is done,
But look forward to the future and what God has in store.
Listen as He says 'for you I have more!'

God You Are Good

God, You are good!
I can hardly believe
You've turned my life around
so totally, completely.
All You asked was that I hold on to You
even when I lay down
and couldn't continue.
You wouldn't let me give up.
You gave me strength
coursing into my being
that I could arise
and continue on.
My Father, my Father,
Your love blows me away,
Your attention just overwhelms me.
There are billions of people on this planet
yet You are concerned about me;
you care about me, my life -
I love You and never want to be without you.

Who Are You?

When asked the question 'who are you?'
What is it that springs to mind?
Is it your passions that state who you are?
Is it your dislikes that make you?
The way you dress?
Or how you style your hair?
What is it that defines you?

Sometimes in life we rush on through,
never taking time to view
what we've become, or even why
we try to smile when we want to cry.
Is it the expectation that we must attain
Man's approval and acceptance our gain?

What do you see when you look at me?
A stranger passes by.
Do you judge by their appearance?
And your opinion formed by that one glance?
Or do you take the time
to go beyond that first look
through the many layers
that make the person before you?

Who am I? I ask myself.
The answer I don't yet know
but this one thing I'm sure of.
I am God's child,
Loved.
If the world falls tomorrow
this one things remains:
I am His!

Perfect Living

I used to think I had to live a perfect life.
As in Proverbs 31, I was that dutiful wife,
finding my worth in the roles that I played.
It was no wonder I became dismayed
for failure was not an option for me.
Bound by conditioning I just couldn't see
living a life that was just an existence,
but God broke through with His persistence
for His word says we are to have a life
abundant and full, although not free from strife,
and so when things went wrong, as often they do,
I thought I was being punished, it just wasn't true.
But such was my thinking, my mindset, my ways,
I tried to be perfect but was sad and afraid,
trapped in a prison of emotions and doubt,
until God came to show the way out.
I was so afraid to make a mistake,
any show of weakness caused me to break,
I felt I had to be strong and never falter,
and my way of living this did halter
living for others in the hope I'd be accepted,
living in fear of being rejected,
finding it hard to ever truly trust,
not really knowing love, only lust,
trying to please those all around
only drove me deeper into the ground,
but thankfully God cares so much for me
he didn't leave me in that place, but set me free,
breaking down barriers I'd built to guard
removing boulders from my life and softening my heart.
I hadn't realised the depths that this went,
and many broken hours of weeping I spent,
as it dawned on me, a victim I'd been
of all that my life was, I had never seen.
As difficult as it was to face these things
the lessons I learned, the peace it brings
my worth is no longer tied to any role.
In this area I believe I'm now whole
no longer living for man's acceptance or love
and for this liberty I thank God above.
Stripped of all I thought I knew,

not knowing if, or how I'd get through,
for there were days I thought I'd die
but in it all God's taught me to rely
upon His love for He'll never leave,
and comfort He brings to those who grieve
'why does He allow suffering?' if such a God of care
exact answers I know not, but my thoughts I'll share.
He has given man a will that is free;
decisions and choices can be made easily.
God will not force us into His way,
but will try to guide us when we begin to stray.
Are our ears open to hear His word?
Are our eyes seeing or is our vision blurred?
I have learned of God in these recent years
learned of His love as He's wiped away tears.
This love He has for us, all thinking defies;
will you believe truth or the master of lies?
For there is an enemy who seeks to end
our lives in all ways, on this you can depend
that our destruction is what he seeks,
and has no conscience of the deceit he speaks
for his end is decided and he has nothing to lose
but you have, so I ask, what will you choose?
A life of freedom in the God of creation
for He has paid for your salvation
making a way through His son on the cross
who considered not Himself as loss
but cried out 'it is done!'
The price for all was paid by one
'for such is My love for you
there is nothing I would not do
you are Mine, if you'd only see
I want you with Me for eternity.'
I dare you to seek the Giver of life,
and I promise it won't be free from strife,
But strength you will find and amazing love,
As God opens the windows of heaven above,
And pours out His blessings on you each day,
You'll be overwhelmed if you chose His way

The latter part of this poem is part of a song I've written called 'Remember Me'

The deceiver

"Your life is over,
your time is past,
you'll never be anything:
come on, 'have a blast'
you've a right to be happy,
to hell with the rest.
It's your life;
you're a long time dead;
do what you want.
Who cares if they condemn?
Don't listen to your conscience,
do your own thing,
look after number one,
happiness it will bring,
you want to enjoy life,
'gaun, have another drink!'"
It's everyone else that's wrong
at least that's what you'll think.

STOP listening to deceit!
Stop listening to lies!
For it'll be your downfall,
it'll be your demise.
It's never too late;
You've never gone too far
that a way can't be found
from where you are
for the God who made you
is calling your name.
Start taking responsibility
and stop looking to blame
your parents, your past,
the things that surround,
but lift up your eyes
and get back on the ground.

Start taking steps
toward the Father
and into His arms
you He will gather
for you are His child
His daughter, His son.
The battle has
already been won -
It's the battle of your mind
that carries on.
Stop listening to the deceiver
and soon he'll be gone!

Red Shoes

I have a pair of gorgeous red shoes
that, when worn, kick off the blues,
and I've kept them good for so many years,
not wanting them worn, such were my fears
it was such a shame for they rarely saw light,
but now they are out, to my delight.
Life is so short to deny simple pleasure,
these little luxuries are like buried treasure.
Once afraid, and I don't know why,
wearing the shoes myself I denied
When I asked myself 'why not?'
no reasonable or decent answer I got
So, out went the box and on went the shoes,
As I walk this life kicking off the blues

Lonely

There are days it's felt more keenly
and yesterday was one of those days.
Driving back through such splendour and scenery,
it assaulted me in so many ways.
At first I didn't realise until
the thought of home assailed me,
then I quickly recognised the foe -
it was the feeling 'lonely'

Ever have that hollow way
just take away your breath?
It seems to suck the life right out
and leave an empty nest.
I tried to push it back,
to maintain my armour,
but yesterday it found me
and right on in it clamoured.

I wept on that journey
and I was surprised
at the emotion that had risen;
tears just blinded my eyes
and yet I am at ease
and quite content within
but yesterday was a battle
that I just could not win.

What was it that I hoped for?
What difference could be made?
As I pondered over this,
this is what I said
'to have a welcome face awaiting
someone glad for my return'
but I knew no-one was waiting
and how my tears did run.

Loneliness can strike when in a crowd
or all alone
and there's nothing to alleviate,
it seems nothing can be done
to shake away this horror,
this feeling that leaves a void.
Oh how I wish it would go away
so I can again be overjoyed

But there is One in whom I hope.
He promises to never leave.
He lifts the weary heart,
and brings comfort to the bereaved.
He takes away our fears
and lifts away our sorrow,
gives us peace for yesterday,
and expectation for tomorrow.

He is the King of Heaven,
the Creator of the earth,
who has longed for us to know Him
since way before our birth.
His heart is ever towards us
if only we could see -
the reason He sent Jesus
was that we might be free

You see it was God's plan
that we were made like Him
that we would walk by His side
and know His peace within,
but satan had a motive,
for man he has such hate,
and it's his desire to keep
God and man separate.

So down into the garden
he came and brought deceit,
for in the game of cunning
he just cannot be beat;
he questioned what God said
and threw doubt into the mind,
and thus sin was born,
and doomed the whole of mankind.

It only took one act
cast out from just one bite;
thankfully God didn't leave it at that
but planned to make it right.
A price had to be paid
for man's downfall you see
so God sent His only Son
to release you and me.

And so it was in Bethlehem,
unto us a child was born,
in a lowly bare stable which
may have seemed forlorn
but God the Father knew
His Son would do the job
over 30 years later
at the hands of jeering mob.

And so Jesus lived His life
in obedience to His Father,
a life so unspectacular, yet
to Him the crowds did gather,
and when the time came
for Him to pay the price,
he bled and died, a sinless man,
while centurions threw dice.

The devil thought he'd won the fight;
mankind was his to play.
What he didn't realise was
God had made a way
for man to redeem himself
and leave behind his sin
by believing in God's son
man could have peace within.

And so with this in mind,
I'll give this loneliness to Him,
for He's already paid for it.
He's paid for ALL our sin.
I am ever grateful
for the love that He has shown
and as I think on these things,
look! – my loneliness has flown…

Swing Seat Thoughts

Lying here on the swing seat,
remembering days of old,
I am so very grateful
God has made me bold.
The fears that held me fast
have been broken and tossed aside
for it's with my Father
that I now abide.

The planes fly overhead
and birds go fleeting past;
wasps and bees, so too flee
and blue-bottles whiz by so fast,
and here I lie wondering why
I never took the time
I had rushed on through my life
mmm.. can't find a word to rhyme.

But I think you get the message -
you know what I'm trying to say:
don't rush on through this life
but take some time today,
to stop and smell the flowers,
or enjoy that setting sun.
This life is to be lived
so go on – have some fun!

The Passing Storm

Lying here
the thunder rumbles in the distance,
the lightning occasional,
there is such stillness.
Only an hour ago
cars revved and raced,
voices shouted drunkenly,
chants and singing,
clatter of cans,
banging of doors,
slamming of gates.
The lightning again,
fleeting.
No sound is heard.
More frequent.
Is it coming this way?
The thunder is silent.
It's almost like creation
is holding its breath,
waiting to see:
Will it strike here?
Or roll past?
Only time will tell.
There are those who sleep,
oblivious to the storm that builds,
turn over and snuggle down.
I lie and wonder
if anyone else is aware?
Are they too wondering?
Will it strike here?
There's a breeze;
It builds
as the lightening flashes.
The thunder rumbles closer.
Will the rain come?
The earth is groaning.
Will the storm satisfy?
Or roll on by?
A plane passes through
It's safe as its altitude is
greater than the storm.

It's low across the horizon.
On the coastline,
I imagine the storm at sea.
The breeze is cooler now,
the temperature drops,
the thunder rolls
are more frequent
and louder.
The lightning covers the horizon
from east to west
and so it goes.
The dry earth
feels no rain
as the storm
so close
passes by
leaving the earth
dry.

Discouraged

It would seem that hope has been lost;
People don't want to count the cost.
It's all about 'me' and 'what I want'
'where is your God?' the enemy taunts,
faced with failure and no fruit from sowing.
It seems there is a desert where nothing is growing
the fields are empty, there's no grapes on the vine,
the olive crop fails and men are blind;
fig trees have no blossoms, it all seems dead,
until the Bible I picked up and read
'the sovereign Lord, He is my strength' it says,
'you have need of endurance in these days'
'hold on tight to the hope that you have'
for there will be days again when you will laugh
'keep your confident trust in God,
for with it will come a great reward'
I try to encourage myself and not give in
Trusting that God will strengthen me within
So when discouraged don't give up hope
But hold on to God, He WILL help you cope!

Doubt

Father, it's strange the way I feel.
I know Your word is true and Your promises are real,
yet there is this doubt that arises in my heart
and I wish I could banish it before it could start.

It brings questions to my mind,
And throws me into space,
And robs the rest in my being,
And causes my thoughts to race.

'How can it be?'
'Is it really true?'
'Time's flying by!'
'Are you sure He meant you?'

Father, I ask, help me when this happens,
for I do not want these doubts for my expectation it dampens.
Help to believe when doubts come round to steal,
help to hold on for I know Your promises are real.

The thoughts of the impossible, I will push right out my head,
and send off the enemy with a card that is red,
He never gives up trying to throw me in a quandary,
and attempts at every turn to thrown up my 'dirty laundry.'

But there's nothing that he has on me that You have not fore-thought
as I stand in Your righteousness, for by Your blood I'm bought
as a 'twig snatched from the fire', my life is in Your hands,
so take away this doubt, that I may walk in Your plans.

Run the race

Help me to run the race
That I shall finish strong

Forgetting what is past
I will press on

Restore my broken places
Redeem this life of mine

That in this world of darkness
Your light in me will shine

And when this life has ended
And I look into Your eyes

I may hear 'well done My child'
This will be my prize

May I be forever watchful
Throughout the course of every day

Laying down my desires
And walking in your way

I cast my cares upon You
Knowing You will not let me fall

That I would not delay
When I hear You call

Thankyou for giving me
The strength when I am weak

And into my ear
Words of comfort speak

And so I ask again
And with this I will be gone

Help me run this race
that I shall finish strong

Let Me Ask...

Who is there like You?
With whom can I compare?
Has there been one who can hold the oceans in his hand?
Or measure the heavens with his fingers like You?
Or know the weight of the earth or even the mountains and hills
Who knows all things but You?
Is there anything that can separate me from Your love?
Can the oceans?
Or the heavens?
Can Your angels?
Or the demons?
Can death?
Can life?
Is there anywhere I can hide from You?

In Response...

My child, I am! I was and I always will be!
I made the oceans and the heavens,
the mountains and the hills.
I know all things including your inner most unspoken thoughts.
I have heard your silent screams and it is time for them to end.
I know all about you, I made you, prepared you and have called you.
Come forth, come forth, the time of mourning is at an end.
Don't be afraid to live! Don't be afraid to live!
Nothing in this life could ever separate you from Me – nothing!
I held the oceans in My hand, but you – your name is engraved on My
hand.
My fingers marked out the heavens – My fingers wipe away your tears
You have been weighed and not been found wanting.
I am coming for you, my bride, be ready!

165

References

The Word For Today
UCB Headquarters, PO Box 255, Stoke-on-Trent, ST4 8YY, England.
Telephone 08456 040401. www.ucb.co.uk/wft
The Word For Today is a devotional produced by UCB free of charge
and are available for the UK and Republic of Ireland

The Power of a Praying Wife, by Stormie Omartian
Harvest House Publishers (2004), ISBN: 0-7369-1407-2

Lord I Want to Be Whole, by Stormie Omartian
STL (2001), ISBN: 0-7852-6703-4

Bishop T.D. Jakes, The Potter's House, 6777 West Kiest Blvd. Dallas,
TX75236. 214-331-0954. www.tdjakes.org

Growing through Divorce, by Jim Smoke
Harvest House Publishers, (1995), ISBN: 1-56507-322-3

Photographs:
All photographs were taken in Scotland, UK

I started on this journey	Glen Rosa footbridge, Isle of Arran
The Beach	Garramore, nr Morar
When I'm here	Loch Long, Sallachy, near Kyle of Lochalsh
Here I sit	Irvine beach, Ayrshire
Alone with my thoughts	Irvine beach looking toward Arran, Ayrshire
Long has been this path	Spring Snow, Ayrshire
Help me to rise	Eve
When I'm surrounded	Loch Long & Ben Kilillan, Sallachy, near Kyle of Lochalsh
Lone Footballer	David Pearson
Lord I'm glad You're in my life	Matt & Kezziah McGregor
The Trees	Hillside trees through Ballachulish Bridge, near Glencoe
Keep it simple	Spring Snow, Ayrshire
Under Cypriot Sky	Pernera Bay, Cyprus
Run The Race	Dick Madden

...forever

Printed in the United Kingdom
by Lightning Source UK Ltd.
118917UK00001B/183-206